Picture the Past
CHESTERFIELD

Picture the Past
CHESTERFIELD

Mike Smith

First published in Great Britain in 2010 by
The Derby Books Publishing Company Limited
3 The Parker Centre, Derby, DE21 4SZ.

ISBN 978-1-85983-874-7

Printed and bound by DZS Grafik, Slovenia.

CONTENTS

Picture the Past: Introduction   6

Acknowledgements   7

Introduction   7

From the Romans to the Glorious Revolution   8

Church and Chapel – Chesterfield at Prayer   16

Students and Scholars – Education in Chesterfield   26

Markets and Malls   35

Riches from the Earth – Mining in the Chesterfield Area   45

Factories and Foundries – Industry in Chesterfield   56

Home Sweet Home – Domestic Housing in Chesterfield   67

From Workhouse to Welfare State – Health and Welfare in Chesterfield   80

Police and Public Order   89

Beer and Skittles – Public Houses and Breweries in Chesterfield   99

Fresh Air and Fun – Parks and Public Spaces in Chesterfield   113

Playing the Game – Amateur and Professional Sport in Chesterfield   124

Footlights and Flea Pits – Theatre and Cinema Entertainment in Chesterfield   138

From Turnpikes to Trains – Improvements in Transport in the Chesterfield Area   145

Trams and Trolleybuses – Public Transport in Chesterfield   157

In Times of Conflict – Chesterfield through two World Wars   167

The New Millennium – Chesterfield Looks Towards the Future   180

Select Bibliography   192

INTRODUCTION

In the past, anyone wanting to view the collections of hundreds of thousands of old images in the libraries and museums of Derbyshire or Nottinghamshire would have had to travel many miles to try and track down the ones they were interested in. This proved to be frustrating and time-consuming for researchers, a barrier to anyone from further afield and damaging to the more fragile images due to all the handling. The collections include photographs, slides, negatives, glass plates, postcards and engravings recalling the history of our local communities over the past hundred years and more.

Thankfully, senior staff in four local authorities got their heads together to solve the problem, and the idea of conserving the images using digitisation, while at the same time giving people all over the world access to the digitised versions, was conceived.

Funding was obtained from the Heritage Lottery Fund at the beginning of 2002, together with additional cash from the four partner authorities, Derbyshire and Nottinghamshire County Councils and the City Councils of Derby and Nottingham. Local studies staff in the libraries and museums started collating images and information ready for inclusion in the project and sent out thousands of letters requesting copyright clearance from the original photographers or their relatives. Nick Tomlinson was appointed as project manager to lead a team of experienced professionals inputting the information into a custom-built database and carefully digitising the images.

The Picture the Past website (www.picturethepast.org.uk) was launched in June 2003 and by the end of 2007 in excess of 67,000 pictures had been added. It now attracts well over 10,000 visitors from all over the world, viewing thousands of pages of images every month. The site is updated on a regular basis and actually gives the user the ability to 'correct' existing information or add more information to those pictures with scant details.

The website is designed to be as easy to use as possible and includes a simple keyword search facility as well as more comprehensive search mechanisms for users looking for images with a particular theme or by a specific photographer. Visitors can print out low resolution copies for their own personal use or study purposes, but for those users wanting to own a top-quality glossy photographic copy the website includes an online ordering service. Thanks to the involvement of the *Derby Evening Telegraph* this enables users to browse the collection and order and pay for their selections securely online. The prints are produced on state-of-the-art equipment and, as a non-profit making project, all the income raised from this service goes back into the conservation and preservation of more original pictures.

This book gives you the chance to sample just a handful of the images contained in the website and it is very much hoped that you will go on to enjoy the rest of the pictures online.

For people who do not have access to the internet at home, or who are not sure where to start, there are computers available for public use in all libraries and the local studies staff are more than willing to help you get started.

The website can be viewed at **www.picturethepast.org.uk**

Picture Website Wins National Accolades

Nick Tomlinson and Robert Gent receiving the SOCITM award in 2007.

Picture the Past continues to go from strength to strength and has won an award in the 2007 Local Government IT Excellence Awards.

The awards, which are organised by Intellect, SOCITM and SOLACE and sponsored by Ericom, highlight the use of best practice in local government and how IT has been used both effectively and innovatively to deliver best-value public services. The judges were impressed with both the originality of the solution and its potential for expansion and emulation. They commended the project team's commitment to utilise technology in order to preserve the region's heritage. The website won the Alan Ball Local History Award in 2004 in recognition of its commitment to local history publishing.

The awards are made every year by the Library Services Trust to public libraries and local authorities who – through books, magazines, websites or any other form of the written word – promote their communities' local history.

Michael Saich, Chairman of the Library Services Trust, presented the award on 19 January 2005. He remarked 'Picture the Past was successful in the competition, with both print and non-print entries gaining one of the main awards. The Trust was impressed by how successfully the partners worked together to create the website and we feel it is important for local authorities to continue to produce publications of such a high standard.'

ACKNOWLEDGEMENTS

Several people have helped me in my research for this book. I should like to express my particular gratitude to the following: John Bennett for information and advice about public transport in the Chesterfield area. Nick Smith for advice and assistance with digital photography. Picture the Past for providing most of the photographs. The staff at Breedon Books for their advice, support and encouragement and for bringing the work to fruition. The staffs at the following libraries, without whom the research could not have been completed: Chesterfield Library, Derby Local Studies Library, Nottingham University Library (Hallwood and King's Meadow sites).

INTRODUCTION

One of the first decisions I had to make when writing this book was to define the area I was going to cover. At the time of the Domesday survey Chesterfield was part of a royal manor which also comprised Newbold, Whittington, Brimington, Tapton and Boythorpe. The mediaeval parish, however, covered an even larger area including Newbold, Dunston, Brimington, Tapton, Calow, Hasland, Temple Normanton, Walton, Cutthorpe, Whittington, Brampton and Wingerworth.

The boundaries of the town were extended several times in the 19th and 20th centuries and today the Borough of Chesterfield includes Brimington and Staveley as well as the town of Chesterfield itself. In my writing and in my choice of illustrations I have focussed on the town of Chesterfield but have made extensive reference to other parts of the existing borough. Where appropriate I have also referred to surrounding areas.

The story of Chesterfield and its people cannot be defined or restricted by administrative boundaries for it is a story which mirrors the history of our nation. The Romans settled here and by the Middle Ages the settlement had become a flourishing market town. It played a vital role in the Glorious Revolution and the growth of democracy. In the 18th and 19th centuries it played a significant role in Britain's Industrial Revolution and in the development of the trade union movement. George Stephenson, the railway pioneer, made his home here and the new railway station has a statue of the great man outside the main entrance. The growth of education is well represented from the establishment of the Tudor grammar school to the ragged school movement and the creation of School Boards.

Chesterfield today is a lively and vibrant community. It has coped better than many towns with the decline in mining and heavy industry. New employment opportunities have been seized, and the people of Chesterfield have embraced the changes and challenges of the 21st century while preserving the best of their heritage.

FROM THE ROMANS TO THE GLORIOUS REVOLUTION

The first inhabitants of Chesterfield were an Iron Age family who created a farmstead in the area now occupied by the parish church. When the Romans marched north they established a small fort on the site. Constructed around AD 50, it is believed that it was built to protect the road which connected larger forts at Derby and Rotherham. This original earth and timber structure was rebuilt on a new alignment around AD 79–80, only to be abandoned in approximately AD 150. Archaeological excavations in the 1970s revealed evidence of this Roman occupation and a number of interesting finds from the dig are displayed in the local museum. Other evidence of the Roman occupation in the area was discovered in the 1980s when a hoard of 140 silver *denarii* was discovered at Morton, near Chesterfield. They were buried sometime after AD 210, the date when the last coin was minted.

There is no archaeological evidence of early Saxon settlement but it seems likely that the new incomers would have established their settlement on or near the site of the Roman fort. Its location on a crossroads encouraged trade and the possible development of a market. Some historians have also suggested the presence of a church on the site but there is no mention of this in the Domesday survey. The first written reference to Chesterfield comes from 955, when it was recorded that King Eadred granted land in the town to Uhtred Child with the right to administer law and the responsibility to build a town and a bridge. The Vikings also settled in the area, and place names such as Netherthorpe and Woodthorpe suggest the existence of Scandinavian farmsteads.

By the time of the Domesday survey (1086) the royal manor of Cestrefeld (Chesterfield) was governed from Newbold (now a suburb of the town). We do not know the size of the population at this time but it was probably fewer than 50, and it is likely that it provided a home for no more than a handful of families. In contrast Staveley was much larger and more important at this time, with a total population of around 150, a church and a priest as well as a mill.

Chesterfield, however, grew rapidly in importance. A document of 1092 described the town as both a manor and a borough in its own right. During the 12th century a market and later a fair was established in the town and by the end of the century a gaol had been built, serving not only the town but the whole of the Scarsdale wapentake. King John founded a leper hospital just beyond the mediaeval town and in 1204 he granted the manor of Chesterfield to his favourite, William Brewer, along with the right to hold two weekly markets and an eight-day fair.

Detail from the window in the parish church showing activities carried out in and around the town during the Middle Ages.

Detail from the window in the parish church showing the Battle of Chesterfield in 1265.

Detail from the window in the parish church showing Tudor Chesterfield, including the charter granted by Elizabeth I, a grammar school boy and typical half-timbered buildings.

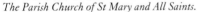

The Parish Church of St Mary and All Saints.

For most of the mediaeval period Chesterfield was untouched by national events, but in 1266, during the conflict between Henry III and some of his barons, a battle was fought in and around the town. Two of the rebel barons, Robert de Ferrers and Baldwin Wake, confronted a Royalist army led by the King's nephew, Henry de Almaine. There was fierce fighting around the church and part of the town was set on fire by the King's men. The rebels, however, were soon put to flight and Robert de Ferrers was taken prisoner. According to one account he was caught hiding in the church among bales of wool stored there by market traders.

Despite this unrest the town continued to grow and expand. New and more substantial buildings were built in the 13th and 14th centuries, including the parish church which was completed around 1400.

The country remained unsettled for a number of centuries with the King, the barons and the church all vying with each other for power. During the Wars of the Roses in the 15th century even the peace of the parish church was disturbed. On New Year's Day 1422, Thomas and John Foljambe led an attack on their rivals who were hearing mass at the time. Local landowners William Bradford and Henry Longford were killed. Henry Pierrepont and Thomas Hailsby were mutilated by having the thumbs of their right hands cut off.

The Tudor period saw a number of changes take place in Chesterfield. Some rebuilding took place, although the layout of the streets remained unchanged. The Falcon Building (previously the Falcon Inn), which now houses the Barnsley Building Society, dates from this period. Tanning was probably the most important of the town's industries at this time, although the cloth industry remained important, and iron workers, shoemakers and lead merchants were also to be found within the town.

The town was also struck by a number of outbreaks of the plague. The most serious of these occurred between October 1586 and November 1587 and claimed the lives of almost 300 people out of a total population of 1,200. Outlying areas do not seem to have been affected; although nine cases were reported in Calow. In some cases whole families were wiped out, and recent research has discovered that around 40 families accounted for 170 or so of the burials during this period. Brimington was struck by the plague in 1603 and two further outbreaks afflicted Chesterfield before the end of 1609. Some families fled the town to escape infection and by the early years of the 17th century it seems likely that the population of the town would have fallen to well below 1,000.

This period also saw an important development in the self government of the town. In 1598 Queen Elizabeth I granted a charter to the town which established a common council (often referred to as the Corporation) to govern the town. This comprised a mayor, six aldermen, six brethren and 12 capital burgesses. Collectively they had the right to make contracts, own property and have a common seal. The Corporation also had the power to enact by-laws necessary for the 'good rule and government' of the borough and were able to enforce these laws by fining or imprisoning those who failed or refused to comply. In many ways the Chesterfield charter was similar to others granted by Elizabeth but it did contain a number of special provisions. These related to the will of Godfrey Foljambe, who had left money to the town to pay for a preacher and a schoolmaster. The charter placed a responsibility on the Corporation to provide and administer a grammar school funded by this bequest.

During the Civil War between the King and Parliament, Chesterfield changed hands on a number of occasions. In October 1642 Sir John Gell, the Parliamentarian commander, entered the town unopposed and raised 200 men before marching on. Early in the following year the Earl of Newcastle, commander-in-chief of the Royalist forces in the Midlands, garrisoned Bolsover Castle, eight miles to the east of the town. In November of that year he marched towards Chesterfield, which was at that time occupied by Parliamentarian forces commanded by Sir Thomas Fairfax. According to a contemporary account, the Royalist forces set fire to the brush on Hady Hill before launching an attack upon the town. Thomas Fairfax's forces fled towards Nottingham, leaving the Royalists to briefly reoccupy the town. Other skirmishes took place

Sir John Gell.

Revolution House.

nearby and in 1644 Staveley Hall was besieged by Parliamentarian forces before eventually surrendering to Major-General Crawford, who captured 12 cannon, 230 muskets and 150 pikes.

The victory of Parliament and the execution of Charles I led in turn to the establishment of a Commonwealth with Oliver Cromwell named as Lord Protector. This was probably welcomed by the people of Chesterfield, many of whom were Presbyterians and supported the Parliamentarian cause. The Restoration of the Monarchy under Charles II resulted in changes to the government of the town, and a number of councilmen who were unwilling to comply with the provisions of the 1661 Corporation Act (under which all holders of municipal office were required to take the Anglican Communion and renounce Presbyterianism) were forced from office.

The town's most significant involvement in national affairs, however, came in 1688 when three conspirators met on Whittington Moor to plot the overthrow of James II and his replacement with William of Orange. The three conspirators were William Cavendish, Earl of Devonshire, the Earl of Danby and Mr John D'Arcy. A shower of rain forced the three to take shelter in the Cock and Pynot alehouse at Old Whittington. It was here that they agreed to send an invitation to William to seize the throne. A coded message was sent to William and plans were laid to raise armies in support of the invasion. In the event James II saw that his cause was hopeless and was allowed to flee the country. William and his wife Mary were installed as joint monarchs and the Earl of Devonshire was rewarded for his part in this 'Glorious Revolution'. Created first Duke of Devonshire and showered with other honours, he was also granted Crown Rights to the High Peak Hundred. The lucrative lead-mining rights associated with this area added to his already considerable wealth and he was able to build Chatsworth House just a few miles to the west of Chesterfield. The Cock and Pynot was later preserved as Revolution House and was purchased by Chesterfield Corporation in 1938. Today it is a museum and is open each year from Easter until October.

Celia Fiennes, a pioneering female traveller, visited the town in 1697 and wrote in her journal: 'the town looks well, the streets good, the Market very large'. At the dawn of the 18th century, however, Chesterfield was still very much just a market town with a population of around 4,000 people. Turnpikes and canals were still to be built. Some industries such as tanning, bell founding and brewing were in evidence, but the transformation of the town into an industrial centre was not to happen for a further century.

Detail from the stained-glass window presented to the parish church in 1984 which shows the Earl of Devonshire, the Earl of Danby and Mr John D'Arcy plotting the 'Glorious Revolution'.

Revolution House, Old Whittington. Revolution House takes its name from the Glorious Revolution of 1688. At that time it was an alehouse, called the Cock and Pynot, and it was here that three local noblemen – the Earl of Devonshire, the Earl of Danby and Mr John D'Arcy – met to begin planning their part in events which led to the overthrow of King James II in favour of William and Mary of Orange.

Revolution House, 1902. Seen here decorated for the coronation of Edward VII.

Interior of Revolution House showing the parlour, 1946.

Revolution House, kitchen interior, c.1970.

King Edward VI, who swept away the chantries in the town.

Queen Elizabeth I, who granted a charter to Chesterfield in 1598.

King Charles I. Charles I stayed briefly at Staveley Hall on two occasions during the Civil War.

King James II. His overthrow was plotted by the Earl of Devonshire, the Earl of Danby and Mr John D'Arcy at the Cock and Pynot in 1688.

CHURCH AND CHAPEL – CHESTERFIELD AT PRAYER

The first church in Chesterfield was probably built during the Saxon period and may have been a 'minster church', evangelising and serving the surrounding area. No church is mentioned in the Domesday account, but a document of 1093 specifically refers to 'the church and manor of Chesterfield' being granted by William II to the Dean of Lincoln Cathedral. The present church was constructed during the 12th and 13th centuries. Generations of local people probably watched in awe as this massive structure rose skywards over a period of almost 200 years. It was built by highly-skilled master masons assisted by their apprentices, with most of the actual work being carried out by lowly-paid labourers earning only a few pennies each week. A huge windlass of the kind used to raise materials to where they were needed is displayed in the town's museum. The church was formally dedicated to St Mary and All Saints in 1233 but the main structure was not completed until the 1370s, and it was not until the early years of the 15th century that the 200ft spire was finally added. It was then, and it remains, the largest parish church in Derbyshire. The parish served by this church extended well beyond the boundaries of the small town and included Newbold and Whittington to the north; Brimington, Tapton and Calow to the east; Walton, Hasland, Temple Normanton and Wingerworth to the south; and Brampton and Cutthorpe to the west.

The church played a vitally important role in people's lives during the Middle Ages. Everyone was baptised, married and buried by the church and the people would regularly visit the parish priest to have their sins forgiven. Every Sunday and church holy day the whole population would attend mass, listen to the sermon and hear news of important events.

The parish church was in many ways the social and economic centre of the community. Housing the chantries of the craft, social and merchant guilds meant that much of the business life of the town was conducted there. The location of the church, adjacent to the old market, also meant that it was customary for the nave to be used for storage and as a meeting place.

Until the reign of Henry VIII the Church of England was part of the universal Catholic Church headed by the Pope in Rome. Henry's desire for a divorce, however, led to the English Reformation and the break with Rome. As in other churches throughout the kingdom, the parish church at Chesterfield was forced to adapt to this new theology. An English translation of the Bible was placed in the church and some changes made to the liturgy. The priest had to acknowledge the King as Head of the Church but in many ways the ordinary parishioners would not have noticed any major changes.

A detail from the window in the parish church showing the building of the church in the Middle Ages.

The Parish Church of St Mary and All Saints.

Holy Trinity Church. This church was built in 1837.

The religious pendulum continued to swing throughout the Tudor period. Catholic traditions and services were briefly restored during Mary's reign but under Edward VI harsher protestant doctrines were imposed, and in 1588 the religious guilds and chantries were swept away. The religious settlement of Elizabeth I brought a period of broad toleration, although Catholics and others were fined if they failed to attend services and Catholic priests could be executed as traitors. Records show that a total of 44 recusants (those refusing to attend church services) from the parish of Chesterfield were prosecuted during the period 1591 to 1641.

The 17th-century conflict between King and Parliament also had a religious dimension and this was reflected in the appointment of the local vicar. In 1653 John Billingsley, a Presbyterian minister, was appointed but following the Restoration of the Monarchy and the passing of the Act of Uniformity in 1662 he was forced to leave. He moved to Mansfield but returned to the town on a regular basis to minister to his puritan followers.

As the population grew and the town expanded a number of other churches were built. These included St Thomas' Church, Brampton (1830) and Holy Trinity Church, Newbold Road (1837). It was here that George Stephenson, the famous railway pioneer, was buried. The parish church of Saint Mary and All Saints was also improved during this period. The famous architect Sir George Gilbert Scott was employed to carry out a programme of restoration, involving the removal of old galleries on all sides of the nave, the replacement of the flat ceiling and the fitting of a new east window. The church pews were also replaced to provide additional seating for the poor.

The vicar responsible for these changes was the Revd Thomas Hill. Unlike many of his predecessors he showed a real concern for the welfare of the poor and in 1831 he organised practical help with money and the distribution of soup to 350 families. Two years earlier he had forbidden the ringing of church bells to mark the opening of the Chesterfield races. He disapproved of the drunkenness and gambling which accompanied them and despite vigorous opposition he refused to back down.

By this time other Christian denominations were well established in the town. This had started when the restrictions which had been placed on Catholics and other dissenters were eased by the passing of the Act of Toleration in 1689. The first nonconformist chapel to be built in the town was the Elder Yard Independent Chapel, which was opened in 1692. This was occupied by a group of dissenting Protestants. A few years later an agreement was made between the Independents and the Presbyterians for its joint use. Other nonconformist congregations established their own places of worship over the next few decades. These included the Baptists,

Elder Yard Unitarian Chapel.

Fire at the Church of St Mary and All Saints, 22 December 1961.

the Armenian Methodists, the Congregationalists and the Quakers. John Wesley, the founder of the Methodist religion, preached in the Market Place in 1776 and again the following year, but the first Wesleyan chapel (in Saltergate) was not built until 1795. The Mormons (the Church of Jesus Christ and the Latter Day Saints) arrived in Chesterfield around 1850 and took over an existing chapel at the top of Soresby Street.

A religious census conducted in 1851 showed the following adult attendances at the places of worship within the town:

St Mary's Parish Church	1,445
Trinity Church	277
Primitive Methodist Chapel	580
Independent Chapel (South Pl)	159
General Baptist Chapel	55
Wesleyan Methodist Chapel	550
Elder Yard Chapel	145
Independent Chapel (Soresby Street)	293
Church of Jesus Christ and the Latter Day Saints	196
Society of Friends	41

The building of the railways and the growth of industry led to an influx of Irish Catholics settling in the town, but it was not until 1854 that the Catholic Church of the Annunciation was opened in Spencer Street. The Salvation Army began its work in the town in 1880, moving to its present hall in 1891, where it has remained ever since. By the early years of the 20th century the Spiritualist Union of Great Britain had also established a presence with two groups meeting in the town. Several new churches were built in the

St Michael and All Angels Church, Brimington.

second half of the 20th century to provide for the expansion of the borough and the overall increase in population. A good example is the new Methodist Church at Staveley, which was built in 1976.

The 20th century also saw near disaster as well as triumph for the parish church. On 22 December 1961 a fire, which started in the organ, destroyed the North Transept and nearly reached the famous spire. Undeterred, three days later the congregation gathered to worship on Christmas Day. Repairs were carried out and today no sign of the fire remains. In 1984 a window was given to the church by the people of Chesterfield to celebrate its 750th anniversary. It traces the history of the town from the 13th century to the present day and confirms the important place which the church has played in the life of the town for much of its history.

St Peter and Paul Church, Old Brampton.

WHITTINGTON CHURCH, DERBYSHIRE.

✠ RICARD : L : E : FJZ : IOHAN

Fig 2

St Bartholomew's Church, Old Whittington, 1789.

P.M. Chapel, Whittington Moor,---ca1905

NADIN'S SERIES

Primitive Methodist Chapel, Whittington Moor, c.1905.

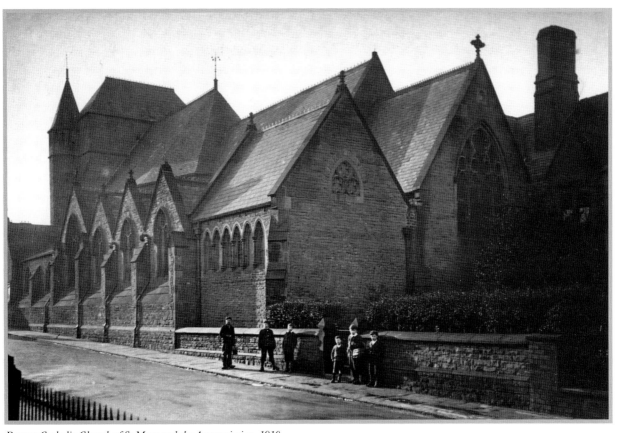

Roman Catholic Church of St Mary and the Annunciation, 1910.

Eyre Chapel, Newbold, c.1800.

St John's Church, Staveley. The Church of St John dates from the 13th century. The north aisle was added in 1865–69 by Sir George Gilbert Scott. The church holds many monuments and tombs of the Frecheville family, the local lords of the manor.

Independent Chapel, Rose Hill, Chesterfield, c.1839.

Bethel Methodist Chapel, Brimington. The Bethel Methodist Chapel was built in the early 19th century but was demolished c.1965.

Salvation Army building, Markham Road, 1997.

The Frecheville Chapel, St John's Church, Staveley.

New Methodist Church, Staveley, 1976.

Students and Scholars – Education in Chesterfield

hesterfield had a grammar school as early as the 13th century. The first record of this school is found in a letter dating from the reign of Henry III in which Henry, a clerk of Ashbourne, wrote to the rector of Chesterfield thanking him for his assistance in securing his appointment as schoolmaster of the Chesterfield School. Other documents from later in the century identify a certain Sir Henry of Sutton as 'master of the schools of Chesterfield'. It seems likely that the school continued under the auspices of the Guild of St Mary and the Holy Cross until the dissolution of the chantries and guilds in the reign of Edward VI.

Chesterfield Grammar School was re-founded in the reign of Queen Elizabeth I. In his will of 24 February 1594, Godfrey Foljambe of Walton left money 'for and towards the fynding of a schoolemaster beying sufficiently learned for the teaching and instructing of children within the town of Chesterfield'. The school was eventually established in 1598 under the charter granted by Queen Elizabeth, and the chapel of St Helen was converted for the purpose.

The school flourished during much of the 17th and 18th centuries. In 1710 the school was rebuilt and Daniel Defoe, who visited the town in 1723, commented: 'The free school in this town is reckoned the most considerable of any in the north of England and sends great numbers of students to the universities, particularly Cambridge'. This was followed by a period of decline and by 1827 there were only five boys in the school. The master at this time was Revd Thomas Field, who was also Curate of Great Barlow and Brimington. He often spent only one or two hours a day at the school and even such attendance was liable to interruption by his parochial duties. He died in 1832 and the school was shut up for some years. The school was rebuilt in 1846 and reopened under the headmastership of the Revd Frederick Calver MA. Under his leadership the school managed to attract increasing numbers of pupils and by 1846 there were 95 scholars enrolled. Latin, mathematics and English grammar were taught at the school, and most boys left at the age of 14.

In the years which followed, various changes were made to the governance of the school and in 1896 two representatives of Derbyshire County Council joined the governing body. By the early years of the 20th century the school was said to be in a flourishing condition with a staff of eight masters. There were 145 boys on roll, of whom 12 were boarders.

It was also during the reign of Queen Elizabeth I that a grammar school was established at Staveley. This was founded by Francis Rhodes of Woodthorpe Hall, one of Her Majesty's Justices. He, like Godfrey Foljambe, also provided in his will for the school. Other

Chesterfield Grammar School, 1911.

Staveley Netherthorpe Grammar School, c.1930s.

The Victoria School, Vicar Lane. The Victoria 'Bluecoat' School was built in 1845 and demolished in 1934 to commemorate Queen Victoria's visit to Chatsworth, and it was attached to the parish church. The pupils wore a distinctive blue uniform paid for by the church.

The School Board offices, Durant Road, c.1900. This was formerly Durant Road Infant School.

bequests included £8 per year from Margaret Frecheville towards the wages of a schoolmaster. The school was closed in 1847 but reopened in 1865 when the charge for tuition was £4 4s 0d per annum, with French, German, drawing and music all available at an extra charge. It remained a small school and the number on roll in 1867 amounted to only 20 day boys and two boarders. It became a mixed school in 1900 and shortly afterwards the Victoria County History reported that: 'There are now 97 boys and girls under Mr Miall Spencer MA with a staff of three masters and four mistresses.'

For most of their lives both these schools provided a classical education for a small male educational and social elite. It was left to the churches to provide elementary education for boys and girls of working-class families. In many areas Sunday schools and ragged schools provided simple instruction in reading, writing, arithmetic and religious knowledge. Large numbers of children, however, continued to be employed in mines, potteries and iron works from an early age, many of whom could barely read or write.

In order to improve standards of literacy, the churches began to establish day schools. The Church of England established the National Society while the nonconformist churches promoted the work of the British & Foreign School Society (known as Lancastrian schools). Both organisations used the monitorial system, whereby the teacher provided instruction to the older pupils, the monitors, who then taught the others.

The Anglican Church in Chesterfield opened the National School in Soresby Street in 1815. This remained the only National School in the town until the opening of the Victoria School in May 1845. Known as the 'Bluecoat' School due to the uniforms provided by the vicar and his wife, this school was also a general centre for all the Sunday schools in the district.

The first nonconformist school in Chesterfield was the Lancastrian School for Girls, more often known as the School of Industry. It was built by voluntary subscriptions and opened in 1819, although it had been in existence for some years before the erection of the new school building. It was founded to 'instruct the female children of the poor in the duties of servants, and in the principles and duties of Christianity'. A report of 1835, however, complained that many of the girls left the school at an early age to be employed in needlework or other sedentary occupations. The establishment of a boys' school followed in 1843 with the opening of the British School in Hollis Lane.

Many children still received their education in petty or dame schools, where they paid fees of between 2d and one shilling each week. According to a government return of 1819, a total of 19 such schools provided tuition for 513 children compared with the 425 children in society and endowed schools.

In 1870 an Education Act gave powers to local councils to establish schools of their own where there were insufficient places provided by voluntary societies. Chesterfield was one of the first boroughs to take advantage of this legislation and the Chesterfield School Board was established in 1871. It identified a shortfall of well over 500 places and quickly set about addressing this deficit. Premises were rented at first but new schools were opened at Hipper Street and St Helen's Street in July and August 1873. Shortly afterwards the board took over the old Industrial School on Durant Road for the nominal sum of £212. According to a local publication of 1882, these schools taught a number of subjects including reading, writing, arithmetic, geography, grammar, literature, domestic economy, drawing, needlework and animal physiology. This same publication lamented the fact that cookery was not taught and commented that, 'many a woman's happiness had been wrecked for life because she could not cook her husband's dinner'!

As a result of the 1902 Education Act, school boards were abolished and elementary education became the responsibility of Chesterfield Town Council, which was constituted the Local Education Authority of the borough. Educationally, Chesterfield has always been something of a pioneer. It led the country by raising the school leaving age to 15 as early as 1933. This was something not even envisaged nationally until the passing of the 1944 Education Act, and the national school leaving age was not actually

St Mary's High School, Newbold Road, under construction in 1980.

raised until 1947. Chesterfield retained control of education in the post-war period and became an Excepted District under the terms of the 1944 Act.

Following local government reorganisation in the 1970s, education became the responsibility of Derbyshire County Council. Over the years considerable changes have taken place in the organisation and structure of education in the town. In 1990 secondary education was reorganised with the creation of just five schools to replace the previous 11. Changes in government policy in recent decades have led to the creation of a number of different types of school, including specialist colleges. Chesterfield Grammar School, for example, moved into new premises in 1967 and was renamed Brookfield Community School in 1990. It is now a specialist sports college with over 1,300 pupils on roll. New schools continue to be built in the borough. Newbold Community School moved into new premises in 2006 and, at the time of writing, work had already started to replace the run-down Abercrombie School on Victoria Street with a modern, environmentally friendly building which, developers claim, will have a zero-carbon footprint. Funded by Derbyshire County Council, the new school will boast an amphitheatre for various activities and performances, an orchard, separate play areas for different age groups, a rainwater recycling system, solar panels and under-floor heating. There will also be more spacious classrooms with storage space, a medical room, kitchen and improved sports facilities.

The town also has excellent facilities for further and higher education. The Chesterfield and Brampton Mechanics' Institute was established in 1841. It grew and evolved over a number of years and in 1984 the Chesterfield College of Technology merged with the College of Art and Design to become Chesterfield College. In 1993 it became the first Associate College of Sheffield Hallam University and now offers foundation degrees in a number of subjects including construction, electrical and electronic engineering and early years education.

The Ragged School, 1988. Its date of construction was 1878 and it was founded for the benefit of the children of Chesterfield who were living and working in poverty. The school seen here became a member of the Chesterfield Sunday School Union in 1879. By 1885 there were 340 pupils and 27 teachers.

The Ragged School Interior, Markham Road, Chesterfield, 1998.

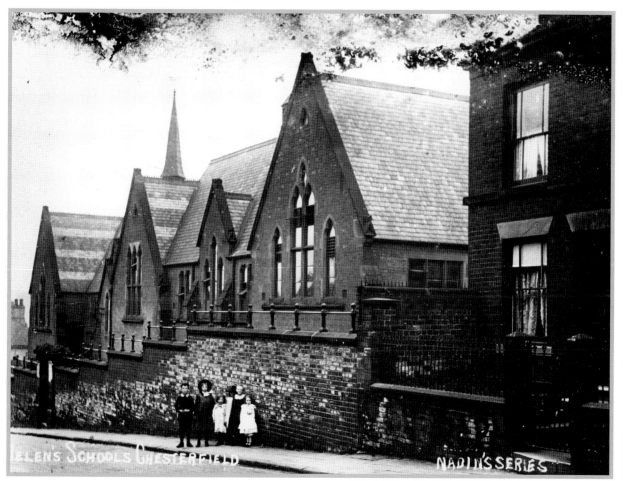

St Helen's School, Victoria Street, 1910 (which later became Abercrombie School).

Mary Swanwick School, Old Whittington, 1907.

Tapton House, c.1902. This was the home of George Stephenson. Later it was home to Charles Paxton Markham, who bequeathed it to Chesterfield Town Girls' School in 1931. It is now part of Chesterfield College.

Pupils at Brampton Board Girls' School taken around 1920.

DCCC002599 – Image Courtesy of J Cutt

Junior Class at New Whittington Primary School, 1925.

DCHQ001669 – Courtesy of Ian N Hill

St Mary's High School under construction in 1980.

Walton Holymoorside Primary and Nursery School, which opened in 2004.

MARKETS AND MALLS

For many hundreds of years Chesterfield was a small, self-sufficient community where people provided for their own needs; growing their own food, weaving their own cloth and sometimes exchanging any surplus which they produced. Eventually a market was established in the town and people from the surrounding villages came to Chesterfield to buy and sell a wide range of goods.

By the late 12th century the town needed a larger market area and a new market place was laid out on its present location. Land on the north and south sides of this new market place was divided into long strips, known as burgage plots, and allocated to the town's householders. As the town grew, distinctive street names were adopted which reflected the businesses sited there. These included Draper Row, Fisher Row, Gluman Gate (the street of the glee men or minstrels), Iron Row, Knifesmith Gate, Mercer Row, Potter Row, Souter Row and Soutergate (shoemakers). The continuing success of the market and Chesterfield's increasing importance as a trading centre resulted in the town becoming more prosperous. This increased wealth allowed for a substantial rebuilding of the parish church in the 14th century.

By the Tudor period Chesterfield's market continued to be the principal source of wealth within the town, but by this time leather working, tanning, iron making and the trade in lead also contributed to the local economy. In addition to the market, a growing number of shops catered for the needs of the townspeople as well as those living in the surrounding areas. These included drapers, mercers, grocers and ironmongers. The Steward of Haddon Hall sent to Chesterfield for a variety of goods and his accounts for this period show that he shopped for rye, veal, mustard, sugar, prunes, raisins, claret, malt, hops, drinking cups and 'all kinds of sea fish'. When Celia Fiennes visited Chesterfield towards the end of the 17th century she found 'a great market like some little faire, a great deal of corn and all sorts of ware and fowls there'. She was pleased with the prices there and declared: 'I bought myself two very good fat white pullets for six pence both, and I am sure that they are as large and as good as would have cost 18 pence if not two shillings apiece in London'. Almost 30 years later Daniel Defoe found a 'very good market, well stored with provisions'.

The Market Place in 1860, from a painting by Nottingham artist W. Smyth.

...g of the railways and the growth of industry led to an increase in population and a growth in the number of shops. ...et, however, remained important throughout this time. A new Market Hall was built in 1857 and a dedicated area for cattle ...es was created away from the main square. At around the same time some of the older buildings around the Market Place were replaced by newer shops.

By the early years of the 20th century a few branches of national chain stores such as Boots the Chemist and Liptons had opened within the town, but most of the shops were still owned by local families. Because of the market, they served the needs of the surrounding areas as well as local residents. There were, of course, no department stores or supermarkets at this time and housewives had to go from shop to shop making their purchases from individual butchers, bakers, grocers, fishmongers, ironmongers or haberdashers. Among other businesses *Bulmer's Directory* of 1895 listed two baby linen dealers, five bakers, 34 butchers, five booksellers and stationers, four chimney sweeps, 12 confectioners, 29 drapers and hosiers, 10 dealers in fancy goods, four fish, game and poultry dealers, 15 greengrocers and fruiterers, five milliners, 18 tobacconists, 25 tailors, clothiers and outfitters and five pawnbrokers, all carrying out their business within the town.

A guide to Chesterfield published in 1899 provides us with a more detailed picture of some of the retail establishments serving the town at that time. The business of Mr S. Hadfield in the Market Place was described as the largest wholesale and pork butcher in the town, whose window frontage displayed 'a tasteful assortment of the choicest joints of dairy-fed pork, home cured hams and bacon'. He also prepared his own 'Chesterfield sausages', polonies, pork pies, tomato sausages, potted meat and brawn. There were a number of drapers, milliners, shoemakers and general clothing stores in the town. Mr S. Swale, the clothier, outfitter and draper on Vicar Lane, sold 'every article of men's, youths' or boys' outfits, from a necktie or a shirt to a suit of ready-made or measured clothing'. Cigarettes, cigars, pipe tobacco and snuff were all popular at this time and a number of tobacconists served the needs of

Mr Herbert Green. Wholesale Tobacco and Cigar Merchant, Holywell Street (from an advertisement of 1901).

smokers (mainly men at this time). Mr Herbert Green's tobacco and cigar business on Holywell Street stocked a wide range of pipes, cigar and cigarette cases and 'the choicest brands of British and foreign cigars, cigarettes, and packet and loose tobacco'. Like most tobacconists of the period Mr Green also produced his own mixture of tobacco which was popular with many of his customers.

Photography was becoming popular at this time and most middle-class homes would have family portraits proudly displayed. This demand was catered for by Messrs Seaman and Sons, who for many years had a shop and studio at the end of the Market Hall. For the middle classes shopping was starting to become a pleasure rather than a chore and a number of cafés were established which allowed ladies to pause from their shopping to enjoy sandwiches or cakes with a cup of tea. Like today, some were located within shops and the Oriental café on the first floor of Woodhead's the grocers on High Street claimed to be handsomely and tastefully fitted and patronised by the best classes. The first Co-operative store in the town was opened in 1894 in New Square, selling groceries and provisions. Within 10 years the society had expanded to supply a wide range of goods including clothing, drapery, crockery, boots and shoes, ironmongery and coal.

In 1910, and again in 1914, shopping festivals were organised to support local businesses, publicise the town and stimulate trade. A wide range of activities were organised on both occasions. In 1914 these included competitions, special window displays, a fair, a grand carnival and a cycle parade of messenger

Chesterfield's first Co-operative Society shop, 1894.

"So clap hands, and a bargain."—Shakespeare.

SHOPPING FESTIVAL PROGRAMME.

Special Attractions of the Week.

ON EIGHT DAYS—FRIDAY, April 24th, to SATURDAY, May 2nd—Tradesmen's Window Dressing Competitive Display. Public Voting for Festival Prizes. The voting card giving the nearest actual result will secure to the voter a First Prize of £10. Other prizes: £5, £2/10/-, and Ten of £1 each.

ESSAY COMPETITIONS open to Boys and Girls attending the Elementary Schools and Ladies residing within 10 miles of Chesterfield for Cash Prizes. (See next page for particulars).

ON FOUR DAYS—WEDNESDAY, THURSDAY, FRIDAY, & SATURDAY, April 29th and 30th, and May 1st and 2nd—Mr. B. C. HUCKS, the famous aviator, will give Exhibitions (weather permitting) of Flying, Upside-down Flying, and "Looping the Loop," for the first time in the Midlands.

THURSDAY, April 30th, Tradesmen's Tableau Turnouts; Decorated Motor Cars and Cycles; Historic and Comic Costumes; Messenger Boys' Cycles; Perambulators and Push-carts; Ambulance Squads; Boy Scouts, etc. (See Special Programme).

ON FOUR DAYS—MONDAY, April 27th, to THURSDAY, April 30th—FREE CINEMATOGRAPH EXHIBITIONS will be given on the Balcony of the Market Hall. The Pictures, in addition to comedy and general subjects, will include reproductions of the work in progress in local factories.

In the Alpine Garden a new electrical device will enable beautifully coloured rays to be continually scintillating after dusk. The arrangement will be one of the most novel and prominent points of light during Festival week.

West Bars will be specially illuminated with high pressure gas lamps.

New Square will be treated with various devices in illumination, both in electricity and gas.

All the Corporation Tram Cars will be specially fitted with coloured lights.

For this week electricity will be supplied to Tradesmen at 2d. per unit, and gas will also be reduced pro rata.

The programme of the 1914 shopping festival.

Knifesmith Gate looking towards the junction of Elder Way. The Co-op Department Store is in the centre.

boys and tradesmen's vehicles. The festival programme also advertised that 'Mr B.C. Hucks, the famous aviator, will give exhibitions (weather permitting) of Flying, Upside-down Flying and Looping the Loop'.

The 1920s and 1930s saw the arrival of a number of chain stores such as Woolworths and Marks and Spencer, and some of the older family concerns began to go out of business. Others, however, survived until well into the second half of the 20th century. Among these were John Turner's drapers shop and Britt's ironmongers, which only finally ceased trading in 1989. It was also during the 1930s that a number of half-timbered shops with colonnaded walkways were built. Nikolaus Pevsner, the famous architecture scholar, condemned this architecture as 'Chesterisation'.

The market continued to be popular and well patronised in the early 1900s. The growth of car ownership in the 1950s and 1960s, however, began to put a strain on the road system within the town and plans were considered to build over the Market Place. Following discussions, these plans were rejected and instead a conservation-based policy was introduced, resulting in the preservation of the frontage of Low Pavement and the addition of a new shopping centre (the Pavements Centre) at the rear in 1981. The trend towards shopping malls led to the opening of the Vicar Lane pedestrian shopping precinct in 2000. Changing trends also saw the building of a number of supermarkets on the edge of the town and the construction of large warehouse-style shops such as B&Q.

Chesterfield continues to attract shoppers from far and wide. The reasons for its continuing success were summed-up in the Borough Plan, which noted that 'Chesterfield town centre has retained its importance as the major focus for shopping, services and community facilities and related activities for people living in the north-east of Derbyshire. Major retail schemes at The Pavements and Vicar Lane have maintained the attractiveness of the centre in the face of increasing competition, particularly from new out-of-centre developments at Meadowhall and the McArthur Glen factory outlet scheme at Junction 28 of the MI. The attractiveness of Chesterfield town centre is partly due to its traditional character, based as it is around a popular market and a range of shops complementing a range of smaller independent shops.'

The challenge for Chesterfield in the future is to accommodate further growth in retail business without losing its traditional character.

Interior of the Pavements Shopping Centre.

Rainforth and Biggin, Packers Row. Grocers and tea sellers. Listed in White's Directory, 1857.

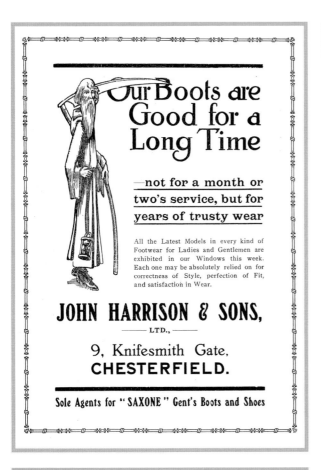

Advertisements from the 1914 shopping festival.

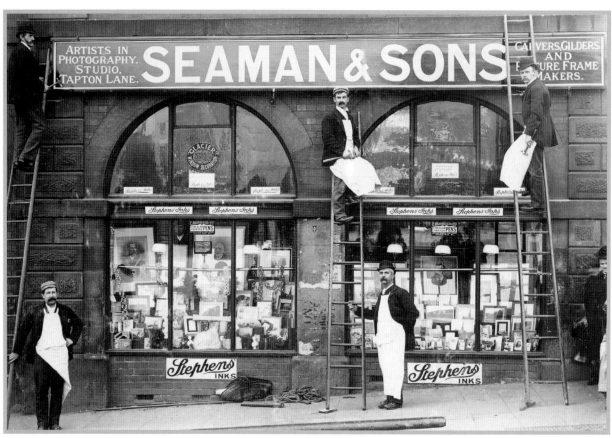

Seaman and Sons photographic shop in the Market Hall, c.1895.

G. Haag's butcher's shop, Beetwell Street, c.1910.

Woodhead's Grocery Store, Packers Row Corner, c.1900.

The Clothing Hall, men's tailor's shop at the corner of Central Pavement and Packers Row, c.1890.

Elliott's Sweet Shop at No. 9, Market Place. Shown in the window is the first prize certificate awarded for the window display during the shopping festival of 1910.

J.B. White and Sons furniture store in Tapton Lane, c.1899.

Riches from the Earth – Mining in the Chesterfield Area

There is some evidence to suggest that coal was mined in the area from as early as Roman times. It seems to have been used as an oven fuel at Chesterfield and may have been mined in the Calow area. It seems likely that mining was carried on in the Middle Ages and a document of 1451 refers to a coal mine at 'Dugmanton'. Coal mining was certainly an important activity by the 17th century, for when Celia Fiennes visited she found 'coale pits and quarries...all around, even just at the town end'. These would have been simple bell pits for she described how 'they make their mines at the entrance like a well and so till they come to the coale, then they dig all the ground about where there is coale and set pillars to support it and so bring it to the well, where by a basket like a hand barrow by cords they pull it up'. By 1800 relatively shallow mines were being worked in places such as Ashgate, Brampton, Boythorpe, Hady, Hasland, Newbold and Whittington as well as other areas to the east of the town.

The development of industry, the increased use of steam power and the growth of the railway system all stimulated the demand for coal. In response a number of substantial coal-mining enterprises were established, including the Clay Cross Company (formerly George Stephenson and Co.). Before long much deeper mines were being sunk and problems such as flooding, suffocation and explosive gases all had to be coped with. Working conditions were hard, with men and boys working long hours in cramped conditions. Accidents and injuries were commonplace and only sparsely reported in the local press.

The 1842 Report of the Royal Commission on the Employment of Children in Mines paints an interesting picture of some of the men and boys who worked in local pits. The following are typical examples:

Tapton
John Kidger
He is 80 years of age and has worked in the pit since he was nine years old. He now does odd jobs on the bank. He is asthmatic and full of pain.

Staveley
William Marson
He is 10 years old and has not worked half a year. He opens and shuts the door and has 8d per day. He goes to the Methodist Sunday School and has been for one year at a day school. He cannot spell but says he can write.

George Jarvise
He is 11 years old and has worked only half a year. He carries garlands on the bank and has 8d per day. He works one week at night, the other by day. He has two miles to walk to the pit and works from seven to five with 40 minutes allowed for dinner. He did nothing before he worked in the pit and never went to church, chapel or school. His mother says she could not make him.

Duckmanton
Samuel Bacon
He is 57 years old and has worked as a collier since he was nine years old. He first headed or assisted an elder brother and had 8d per day, and he has since worked at everything belonging to a pit. For the past nine months he has been quite unable to work owing to asthma. He has had it for two years and attributes it to the 'sweet damp' and gunpowder smoke settling in his lungs. He never used his time regularly to work more than 10 hours a day and considers that it is a long time to be underground...When he was about 24 he was burnt by wildfire and was blinded for a month and he lost his nails. About three years since the roof fell in and broke his breast bone.

The coal was hewed mainly by adult miners using pick and shovel. Most of the seams were between 3ft and 5ft in height but at Brampton the report states 'the seams are so thin that several have only 2ft headway to all the workings'. Here the pits were 'altogether worked by boys'.

New mines continued to be sunk in the late 1800s. In 1882 the Staveley Company leased 5,000 acres of coal reserves on the Sutton Estate from William Arkwright, and by 1885 the new Sutton Estate Colliery, later named Markham Number One, was in full production. A year later, a new shaft was sunk into the Clay Cross Softs seam at a depth of 1,512ft, and this colliery became known as Markham Number Two. The expansion of mining also led to the growth of trade unionism and the Derbyshire Union of Mineworkers was formed in 1887 with its headquarters in Chesterfield. The Staveley Company, however, believed in a policy of benevolent paternalism and was opposed to union membership.

Coal mining in the 19th century. From the 1842 Royal Commission Report.

Picking coal during the General Strike of 1926 at Markham Colliery.

Lowgates Feeding Centre, Staveley, 1926.

The period between the two world wars marked a decline in the coal industry and a reduction in the price of coal. The General Strike of 1926 was called to prevent a cut in miners' wages. In Chesterfield there were few incidents of violence or unrest; although a report in the *British Worker* (a TUC newspaper) provided the following account of the situation in Chesterfield:

'The strike is spreading in the Chesterfield area, and a number of potteries closing down. Some of the men came out in sympathy, while others were stopped because of the shortage of coal and the lack of transport facilities. The Corporation tramway service has been reduced to the running of one car manned by inspectors. Bus services have been increased and this led strikers to issue notices: "Please do not ride on the buses. Blackleg labour. Thank you". The conduct of those on strike continues to be exemplary.'

The relatively peaceful nature of the dispute in Chesterfield was probably also due in part to the attitude of the authorities. The police behaved in a tactful and non-confrontational manner and the town council provided concerts and sport in the parks to keep the striking workers occupied. As a consequence there was only one serious incident of disorder when on 10 May a lorry laden with coal slack was waylaid at Engine Hollow on Newbold Moor by a crowd of about 30 men. When the lorry refused to stop the ringleader smashed the windscreen with a stick.

The strike lasted only nine days but the miners remained out for a further six months until starved back to work. Feeding centres were established in the area and most of the miners were forced to apply to the Board of Guardians for food vouchers, the cost of which would eventually have to be repaid. There were around 500 cases of distress in the area and one ex-miner later recalled hungry men who had walked miles to seek relief, fainting as they waited for their details to be taken down by overworked clerks.

Working conditions remained primitive during the inter-war years. Canaries were still used to detect gas and pit ponies continued to be used for haulage underground. Fatal accidents were commonplace and there was little in the way of compensation for loss of life or injury. The 1938 Markham Colliery disaster, however, was exceptional and stunned the whole country. There were 171 men working on the nightshift on 10 May when an explosion ripped through the colliery, killing 79 men and causing severe injury to 40 others. The explosion was caused by a runaway tub-train which ran off the rails and damaged a power cable, igniting the subsequent cloud of coal dust. Twenty-four of those killed came from the village of Duckmanton, including a father and two sons who died together side by side. A disaster fund was established which raised a total of £51,694 and enabled compensation grants to be paid to the injured as well as payments for marriage allowance, education grants and funeral grants for every disaster widow. Further improvements in safety and working conditions followed nationalisation but mining remained a dangerous occupation, and in 1973 disaster struck the Markham Colliery again. On 31 July, 18 coal miners lost their lives and further 11 were seriously injured when a cage carrying the men plunged to the bottom of a mine shaft. A subsequent enquiry determined that the accident was caused by metal fatigue.

'Snap', the Ireland Colliery pit pony, with her handler S.W. Hinchcliffe after winning first prize in a competition in 1924.

Staveley Markham Rescue Team, c.1930s.

The 1970s and 1980s were marked by industrial unrest and a further decline in the coal industry both nationally and locally. National strikes in 1972 and 1974 resulted in victory for the miners but a decade later the economic and political scene had changed. In an attempt to prevent pit closures the National Union of Mineworkers called for a national strike. But this time the government was well prepared. Large amounts of coal had been stockpiled and police from all parts of the country were deployed to ensure that many pits remained open. In the Chesterfield area there were clashes between police and pickets but the town rallied round to support the miners.

Neither side was prepared to give way and the strike continued until 5 March 1975 when the miners eventually acknowledged defeat and returned to work. In the years which followed one pit after another was closed. Today there are no deep mines in the Chesterfield area and the young men of the town no longer have to go down the pit to earn their living. A few years ago a group of Chesterfield teenagers interviewed retired miners as part of a youth project. One of them wrote: 'The pits are gone but the strength and spirit of our people will remain.'

Ireland Colliery shortly before its closure in 1988. The colliery was opened in 1875 and was owned by the Staveley Coal and Iron Company. The Poolsbrook Country Park now stands on the site.

Ireland Colliery Band marching along Chesterfield Road, Staveley, 1945.

Mr Bygreaves shovelling coal at the Ireland Colliery fire hole in the mid-1950s.

Underground transport at the Ireland Colliery, Poolsbrook, 1950s.

Markham Colliery in the 1930s.

THE STAVELEY COAL AND IRON CO. LTD.

MARKHAM NO.1 COLLIERY.

THIS BLOCK OF COAL WAS CUT OUT
OF THE TOP HARD SEAM DECR.
1908. FOR THE MINING EXHIBITION
AT MALMO SWEDEN 1909.
DIMENSIONS 72·32·42·
WEIGHT 3½ TONS.

Markham No. 1 Colliery – This block of coal was cut for the mining exhibition in Malmö, Sweden, in 1909.

The Derbyshire Miners' Offices, Saltergate, Chesterfield, c.1900.

the town it cited advantages such as cheap electricity, a skilled labour force, good communications, efficient public services and cheap rates. Many of the existing firms expanded and flourished during this period. Robinson's marked their centenary in 1939 by organising a day excursion to London for the whole workforce and their families.

The disappearance of the coal industry and the decline of some of the businesses dependent upon it has had a serious impact on employment in the area. In recent years a number of Chesterfield's manufacturing companies have also closed down, downsized, diversified or relocated. The Bryan Donkin works was finally demolished in 2008. The site of Markham and Co. is now a private housing estate, and the site of Chesterfield Cylinders is now the Alma Leisure Park. Other firms which have closed down in recent years include Dema Glass and Trebor. At Staveley the Devonshire Chemical Works was closed down in a piecemeal fashion over a number of years. The chlorine plant was shut down in 2005 and shortly afterwards the production of sulphuric acid ended. Commenting on the final closure of the works a local councillor said: 'In its heyday I think it earned a place in the town because there were so many people employed there. But it has dwindled away over the years and its safety record has caused a lot of concern to residents. The vast majority of people I have spoken to are glad to eventually see the back of it.'

But the people of Chesterfield have adapted well to changing economic circumstances. They have learned new skills and have taken advantage of new employment opportunities. Some long-standing businesses have survived by adapting to change. The service sector has become more important and the growth of information technology has also provided employment for people in the area. In the 1960s the Accountant General's Department of what was then the General Post Office was relocated to Chesterfield, bringing around 1,000 jobs to the town. A massive office block was built to accommodate those workers but unfortunately it developed serious cracks in its structure and had to be replaced by a new building. Tourism too is becoming more important and in 2002 a new octagonal-shaped tourist information centre was opened close to the parish church, in the same area that was once home to some of the town's earliest craftsmen and traders.

Robert Strachan's Rope Works, Holywell Street, c.1899.

Mason's tobacco factory.

Robinson's Works on Chester Street. Robinson's were makers of packaging and healthcare products.

Robinson's Holmebrook Works, 1913. The photograph was taken prior to the rebuilding in 1914.

An aerial view over Chesterfield Tube Company, 1958.

The 'German Crane' at Markham's Works (Broad Oakes Foundry), c.1900. This photograph shows the German-built cantilever crane. It was installed in 1906 and dismantled in 1955.

Frederick's Ice Cream.

Some of the historic machinery still in use at Clayton's Tannery, 2004.

A general view of the Staveley Works.

Molten iron or steel being tapped from the blast furnaces at night in Staveley Works.

Molten pigs of iron or steel in Staveley Works.

Staveley Works' Sentinel Diesel Hydraulic Shunter and its driver, Bob Straw. The shunter would pull molten iron or hot slag wagons.

Devonshire Works, Barrow Hill, 1905.

The Woodhall-Duckham Plant at Staveley Works. This plant produced a chemical called phthalic anhydride, which was used in paint and coating. It was shut down in the early 1970s, and had been demolished by 1980.

New Postal Finance Department, West Bars, 1999.

HOME SWEET HOME – DOMESTIC HOUSING IN CHESTERFIELD

The original Saxon settlement at Chesterfield was home to only a small group of families. They would have lived in simple houses that were little more than small, rectangular wooden huts with a thatch or turf roof. Archaeological evidence from elsewhere in the country suggests that they may have had sunken floors, a shallow pit over which a plank floor was suspended. The pit may have been used for storage but it is more likely that it would have been filled with straw for winter insulation. Typically, these houses comprised only a single room with a hearth for cooking, heating and light. At certain times of year the accommodation may have been shared with the animals owned by the family. There would have been little in the way of furniture and the family would have slept together.

By the later Middle Ages houses were still largely timber structures with thatched roofs. By this time some of them were two stories high and the houses of merchants and craftsmen also served as shops and workshops. The Shambles still retains the street layout which would have been evident at this time.

During the 16th and 17th centuries many of the mediaeval houses were rebuilt in a more modern style. Sadly these too were swept away in a further period of rebuilding in the 18th century. A significant exception, however, is a half-timbered building which still stands in Low Pavement. Dating from around 1500, it may have been used for a time as a guild hall. Later it was converted into separate tenements. In the 17th century part of the building was used as a shop selling a range of items including sugar, tobacco and gunpowder. It was also during this period that the first map of Chesterfield was drawn by William Senior. Based on a survey of 1610 it shows a small town with most of the houses still clustered round the church and the Market Place.

The Georgian era saw continued growth of the town. No grand terraces or crescents were built in Chesterfield but a few elegant town houses were built as well as some lodging houses. Little remains of Chesterfield's Georgian buildings; although a small Georgian terrace still stands in Saltergate as well as one or two individual properties which have since been converted into offices or business premises.

Georgian houses on Sheffield Road. This photograph was taken in 1938 by the council prior to the buildings' demolition.

Allport Terrace, Barrow Hill, c.1930s. Allport Terrace was built c.1880 by the Midland Railway for its workers.

The development of mining and heavy industry in the area created a need for more housing. Some was provided by local speculative builders but mine owners, industrialists and the railway companies also provided houses as an incentive to recruit and retain the growing number of workers that they needed. At Barrow Hill, Staveley, Richard Barrow built 247 houses in blocks of three. Each of these well-constructed stone cottages had a living room, a scullery and three bedrooms. On the top of the hill he also built a small number of larger and more substantial houses for his managers. But Barrow also had a real concern for the physical, intellectual and moral welfare of his workforce. In the years which followed he also provided a Church of England church and national school, a mechanics' institute and a workmen's dining hall. Although an Anglican himself, he also provided premises for the Primitive Methodists' meetings. Later, his successor, Charles Markham, also developed a new estate for his workers at Brimington.

The development of the railways and later the construction of a municipal tram system allowed people to commute to work and an increasing number of new homes were built in the expanding suburbs of the town.

The conditions in which many people lived, however, was far from satisfactory. In 1892 a report by Dr Barwise, the county medical officer of health, described the housing in the 'dog kennels' (an area between Low Pavement and the river) as overcrowded and unfit for habitation. A large number of these houses only had one bedroom, which was occupied by grown-up families with members of both sexes. These houses could not be put into a sanitary state, and so the only remedy was to condemn the area. Most of these buildings were removed in 1912 when Markham Road was built, and the others were demolished in 1914 when Tontine Road was built between Low Pavement and the Cattle Market.

Conditions were little better in the outlying areas, and in 1909 Vincent Smith, the borough surveyor, described New Bridge Street in Old Whittington (then outside the borough) as follows:

'Road bottomed with brick bats originally, in which deep gutters have been washed through into the clay – surface of road made of house refuse and ashes. Path a series of steps and dangerous. Two steps at a time in one or two places. No gullies nor channels – heap of ashes and garbage laid on street. Back yards: 6ft of brick paving and then ashes and filth as before – pigeons, hen houses and then ash pits and privies.'

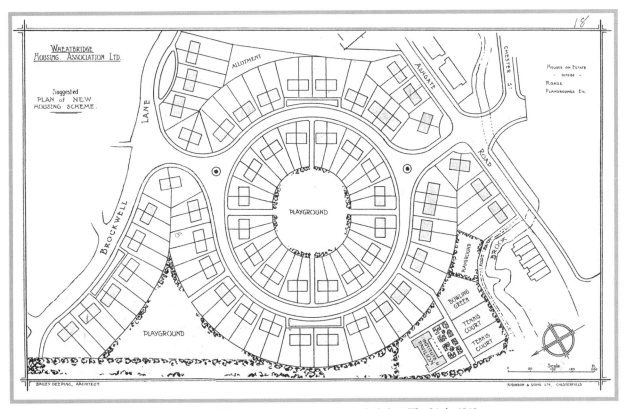

Plan of the new housing scheme proposed by the Wheatbridge Housing Association Ltd, from The Link, *1919.*

One of our Directors is keen on the New Housing Scheme,
In fact our Artist understands that he is to help in building
the first !

Cartoon from The Link, *1919, commenting on the new housing scheme.*

By the start of the 20th century the structure of housing in Chesterfield was similar to that found in equivalent towns throughout the country. The poorest housing was to be found close to the centre of the town in overcrowded yards, intermingled with small workshops and often lacking adequate sanitation. Rows of terraced houses with small back gardens and outside toilets were the homes of better paid working-class families, while the business and professional classes could afford to live in the more spacious villas which were being built on the outskirts of the town.

Following World War One the government promised homes fit for heroes, and in 1919, following the passing of the Addison Act, the council received approval for the construction of 26 workmen's houses on the St Augustine's Road site. It was here and in estates at Boythorpe, Springfield, Racecourse, Barker Lane and Highfield Hall that most of the council-house building took place between the wars.

Robinson's also made a valuable contribution to the town's housing stock in the period after World War One. According to a recent history, the company was responsible for 'creating a small estate of decent semi-detached houses in good-sized plots, built with such an eye to quality that these same houses remain sought-after to this day'.

But many people still lived in sub-standard accommodation. As late as 1923, Brewery Yard, Brampton still had only one communal stand pipe to supply water to 11 houses. In the 1930s the council embarked on a further clearance programme to demolish some of the older yards and alleys in the centre of the town which were no longer fit for habitation.

By the outbreak of World War Two the council had constructed 2,561 houses and this same period had also witnessed a considerable increase in private house building. To encourage home ownership, the borough council provided mortgages to residents seeking to purchase their own house.

Chesterfield did not suffer any significant damage during World War Two but in the years which followed, the population began to increase and the council responded by embarking on a widespread programme of house building. In particular new estates were built in the suburbs. The majority of these post-war estates comprised detached and semi-detached houses incorporating green spaces and community facilities. This programme continued for a number of decades and in the 1960s, when the Department of the Accountant General relocated to the town, a new estate at Loundsley Green was built to accommodate the workers.

The 1970s saw a change in government and the introduction of the 'Right to Buy' policy. This enabled many council tenants to buy their homes at a considerable discount. In the years which followed with increased prosperity and the easily availabile mortgages, owner occupation became the norm. The major house-building firms responded by constructing a wide range of properties in Chesterfield's suburbs, and since this time most new housing has been provided by the private sector.

Many of these new house buyers were affluent singletons, and the latter years of the 20th century saw an increase in the number of starter homes, flats and apartments being offered for sale. In some areas redundant factories and warehouses were converted into luxury apartments. At Chester Street, Brampton, for example, the redundant Robinson's buildings have been converted into flats.

The borough still has a role to play, however, in the provision of a wide range of rented accommodation. The council currently manage approximately 10,000 properties throughout the borough including houses, flats, maisonettes, bungalows and sheltered schemes. The aim is to provide suitable accommodation to meet the needs of all sections of the community.

Robinson's Old Works, Chester Street, Brampton, photographed in 1989, after being converted into flats.

Whittington Hill, Old Whittington, 1907.

Thatched cottages at the top of Boythorpe Road, 1910.

Houses on the north side of Saltergate, c.1900. This photograph shows the entrance to the yard leading to the sawmill.

Newbold Road in 1905.

Houses on King Street, Brimington, c.1904.

Middle-class homes on Ashgate Road, c.1910.

The 'Dog Kennels'. The Dog Kennels area of Chesterfield was located in the present-day Markham Road area. The housing was old and housed mainly Irish families, and they were overcrowded and insanitary dwellings. Most of the Dog Kennels area was demolished in 1912 when Markham Road was built, and the remainder went in 1914 when Tontine Road was built from Low Pavement to the Cattle Market.

Devonshire Cottages, Barrow Hill, c.1930.

The building of council houses at Park Road around 1936. The houses were built on land formerly known as Brown's Tip.

Highfield Cottage, Highfield Road. The photograph was taken in 1939 prior to the cottage's demolition by the council.

Council houses on Maynard Road, St Augustine's Estate, c.1930.

New houses on St Augustine's Avenue in the 1950s. Note the old-fashioned TV aerials and limited parking space.

Local Authority housing, Wythburn Road, Newbold, 1957. Note the provision of open space and a children's play area.

Lordsmill Street in the 1930s. At the time most shopkeepers and their families lived above their shops.

This row of old buildings off Saltergate show signs of being altered at different periods. It appears to have been extended during the Victorian period with an ornate door surround and decorated barge board. The buildings were demolished in the late 1920s to construct Elder Way and to create space for the Co-operative Society building.

Shepley's Yard, Knifesmithgate, c.1900. Note how workshops and houses are clustered together.

Bateman Brothers Removal Firm, Sheffield Road, Chesterfield, c.1899.

From Workhouse to Welfare State – Health and Welfare in Chesterfield

For hundreds of years the church in Chesterfield was the most important organisation providing for the poor, the sick and the elderly. Various guilds (most of them religious organisations) also supported their members during times of hardship. A leper hospital was also established on the edge of the town towards the end of the 12th century. Like other mediaeval hospitals, this was a religious rather than a medical institution, concerned with care rather than cure.

After the Reformation the care of the poor was placed in the hands of parish officials. In order to avoid having to approach the parish, many people joined friendly societies to protect themselves against the worst effects of family illness or death. At the end of the 18th century there were 10 such societies in Chesterfield, with a combined membership of around 800. As the population was only about 4,000 at the time, this was clearly an important safety net for many people. Despite this, many people were forced to approach the Overseers of the Poor when they fell upon hard times as a result of illness, old age or bereavement. Some were given out-relief and were allowed to remain in their own homes, supported by regular weekly payments or by occasional gifts in cash or kind. Others, however, were not so fortunate and were forced to enter the workhouse. A workhouse had existed at Chesterfield since 1737. Situated on the south side of the Bowling Green at the south end of the Market Place, it catered for a maximum of 50 inmates. In 1797 it was described as 'clean and sufficiently spacious with eight or more beds in each room, each filled with chaff and supplied with two sheets, a blanket and a coverlet.' The women were engaged in spinning lint and wool for household consumption, while the men were sometimes sent out to work in the neighbourhood. A report of 1832 described the building as 'commodious' for its 30 residents.

Following the Poor Law Amendment Act of 1834, the Chesterfield Poor Law Union formally came into existence on 19 October 1837. The new Board of Guardians decided that the existing workhouse was adequate for the immediate needs of the union but began to make plans for a new workhouse, which they hoped would 'not have the appearance of either a prison or a palace.' It was also their intention that the new workhouse should be 'an asylum for the aged, the helpless and the infirm', while at the same time it should 'not hold out any inducement to the idle and profligate to enter within its walls'. Work proceeded quickly and the new building received its first inmates on 9 December 1839.

People were admitted to the workhouse for a number of reasons: some were orphans but the workhouse also provided board and lodging for those who, by virtue of old age, sickness, infirmity or desertion, were unable to support themselves. A few were able-bodied paupers who were unable or unwilling to find work. For a number of years they were employed in the crushing of limestone and cinders for road making. Bone crushing for the manufacture of fertiliser and paint was also carried out in the workhouse. The diet of the inmates was dull and repetitive and dinners comprised mainly bread, boiled beef, potatoes and suet pudding. Occasionally, however, the inmates rebelled

DCCC001412 – Image Courtesy of Courtesy of the Derbyshire Times

Scarsdale Hospital, Newbold Road. Formerly the Chesterfield Union Workhouse, it was built in 1838 and replaced the overcrowded workhouse in South Street.

Ashgate Industrial School, c.1906. The Chesterfield Union Industrial School was built around 1880. It was built to house destitute children from the workhouse. It later became a county council residential home for the elderly and was demolished in 1956.

against their conditions. In January 1841, for example, a number of female inmates went on strike when provided with bread and cheese instead of the soup they had expected. As a consequence the governor locked them in the refectory hole until they promised not to offend again.

A report of 1866 painted a grim picture of life in the workhouse. The Poor Law inspector, Mr R.B. Cane, pointed out a number of deficiencies and in one ward he observed, 'seven small children eating their dinner on the floor. They were in a dirty, neglected and discreditable condition.'

The workhouse remained open until well into the 20th century and fulfilled a number of functions. It was in part an orphanage, an old people's home or hospital, and, for a minority, it was a temporary residence during a period of unemployment. But for many of those who spent time there the stigma and shame remained for the rest of their lives.

For many years the care and treatment of the sick also relied on charity. During the early years of the 19th century the poor in Chesterfield relied on the services of a dispensary, which eventually developed into Chesterfield's first hospital. This was opened in 1854 in a small house in St Mary's Gate and catered mainly for outpatients. Its records show that only 13 inpatients were treated in its first year of existence. Of these three died and 10 were cured. It employed a dispenser, on a salary of £25 per year, but no doctors as local general practitioners provided medical treatment on an honorary basis. Within a few years it became obvious that these premises were unable to cope with the demand for hospital care. In 1859 the foundation stone of a new hospital was laid. When completed, the Chesterfield and North Derbyshire Hospital and Dispensary comprised two wards, a small operating theatre and a dispensary. A resident house surgeon was appointed but the day-to-day management of the hospital was left in the hands of a matron. Her duties were described as follows:

'She shall regulate the duties and see to the good conduct of the nurses and servants, over whom she must consider herself the responsible mistress, and shall report to the house visitors or the secretary any instance of neglect or misconduct of the nurses or servants. She shall not discharge nor engage any without the sanction of the board or house visitors, but shall have the power instantly to suspend any nurse or servant guilty of wilful neglect or improper behaviour'.

She was also expected to keep an inventory of all the household furniture, linen and beds and keep an account of all provisions and other articles (except medicines) that came into the hospital. She was further required to 'visit the wards frequently every day, and see that the patients regularly take the medicines prescribed for them'.

The growth of industry in and around the town led to an increase in accidents, and the need for extended accommodation became all too apparent. In 1873 the Devonshire Ward, named after the Duke of Devonshire, a generous supporter, was opened. Further improvements and developments took place in the closing years of the 19th century and in 1900 Alderman Edward Eastwood bought the Durrant Road Board School buildings and had them converted to create two medical wards. He also donated land for the construction of a nurses' home. The number of patients treated in the hospital increased steadily in the years leading up to

Front view of the hospital (1860). Taken from the Chesterfield Hospital Souvenir Handbook, *1917.*

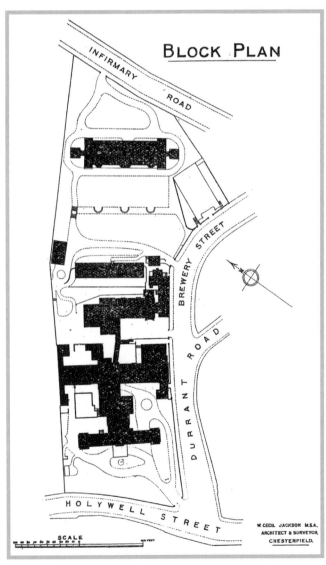

BLOCK PLAN

INFIRMARY ROAD

BREWERY STREET

DURRANT ROAD

HOLYWELL STREET

SCALE

W. CECIL JACKSON M.S.A.
ARCHITECT & SURVEYOR,
CHESTERFIELD.

A Ground Plan of the hospital from 1917.

World War One. In 1913, 1,212 patients were admitted, 1,253 operations were performed and 3,940 outpatients were dealt with. In addition a total of 1,593 casualty cases were treated.

World War One placed a considerable strain on the hospital. Several members of staff were called-up for active service and at the same time income from various workmen's compensation schemes was considerably reduced. The hospital was also expected to play its part in treating the thousands of wounded soldiers who were being shipped back from the battlefields of France and Belgium. As a consequence, the hospital restricted itself to dealing only with urgent local cases so that it could care properly for military casualties. In 1919 the King gave his permission for the hospital to adopt the title Chesterfield and North Derbyshire Royal Hospital.

Throughout its history the hospital was financed by voluntary contributions as well as generous donations from local landowners and industrialists. A considerable amount of money was raised by local groups and charities such as the Women's Medical Ward Fund, the Linen Guild and local churches. Flag days were held to raise funds and a carnival was held each year in Queen's Park.

Patients continued to have to contribute towards their care in one way or another. Many made regular payments through the firm at which they worked while others made direct contributions to the hospital. Those who could not afford to make regular contributions could still receive treatment but had to obtain a letter of introduction from some person of standing such as a clergyman, magistrate or benefactor of the hospital.

During this period, however, most people were treated not in hospital but by local doctors. Arthur Court, who joined his father's medical practice in Staveley in 1889, provides an interesting account of his work in the early years of the 20th century:

'In my early years as a doctor I did a great deal of my work on foot, or in the saddle, although the dog-cart was an occasional luxury…Chesterfield Hospital only received surgical cases then, and except for injuries admission was not freely available as it is today. This meant that the country doctor had to undertake many operations in the homes of his patients that he would not dream of doing today.

'Many infectious diseases such as smallpox and typhoid fever, which are now looked upon as almost extinct, were of common occurrence. I recollect more than one serious outbreak of smallpox in Staveley…in which a number of people lost their lives. All these people were treated in their own homes for there was no fever hospital then.'

The creation of the NHS in 1948 transformed the treatment and care of the sick by providing free medical, dental and hospital treatment as well as eye tests and free spectacles for those who needed them. This, together with improvements in medical knowledge, resulted in an increased demand for hospital treatment and it soon became evident that the existing hospital could no longer cope with a growing number of patients. Land had been purchased in Ashgate in 1945 but it soon became clear that

An advertisement for Lote's Little Life Drops, 1920. Many people took patent medicines at this time as a visit to the doctor could be expensive.

any new hospital would be better located to the east of the town, close to the motorway. A suitable site at Calow was identified and on 29 April 1984 the new Chesterfield & North Derbyshire Royal Hospital NHS Trust opened its doors to patients. The hospital was officially opened by the Queen the following year and in 1986 work began on the maternity and gynaecology department. When this opened in 1989 the old facilities in the town centre were finally closed.

With a staff of around 2,500 and a budget of over £75 million, the hospital provides the most modern facilities for the benefit of the people of Chesterfield. A far cry from the original hospital which opened its doors in 1854!

The Board of Guardians outside their offices (c.1890–1900). Chesterfield Poor Law Union formally came into existence on 19 October 1837, and its operation was overseen by the elected Board of Guardians.

DCCC001324 – Image Courtesy of Seaman and Sons photographers

Board of Guardians' offices, Newbold Street, 1994. Built in 1895 for the Board of Guardians of the nearby workhouse, its later uses include being the Area Education offices.

The Infirmary, Chesterfield.

Chesterfield Infirmary in 1905.

Chesterfield Ambulance, c.1916. This is a Wolseley ambulance believed to have been presented to the town in 1916. It was the first horseless ambulance in the area.

Chesterfield Royal Hospital, Holywell Street, in 1885.

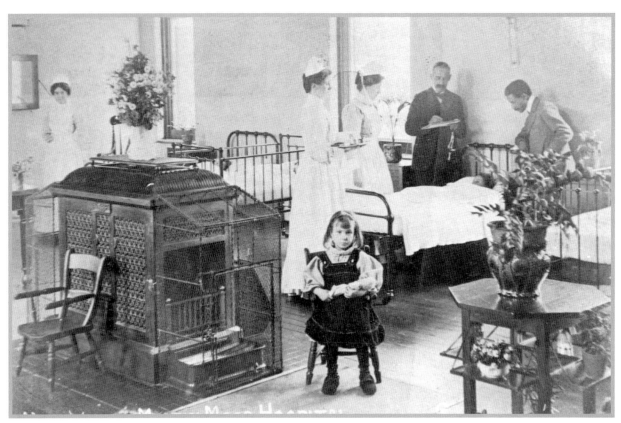

Mastin Moor Hospital, No. 1 Ward, c.1900–10. Mastin Moor is a small village lying just east of Staveley.

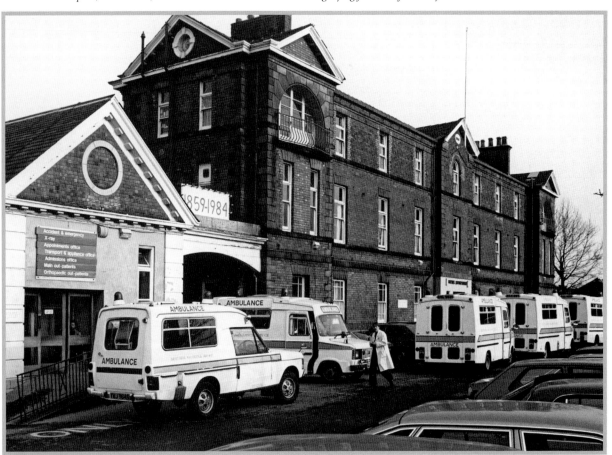

Chesterfield Royal hospital's main entrance, 1984.

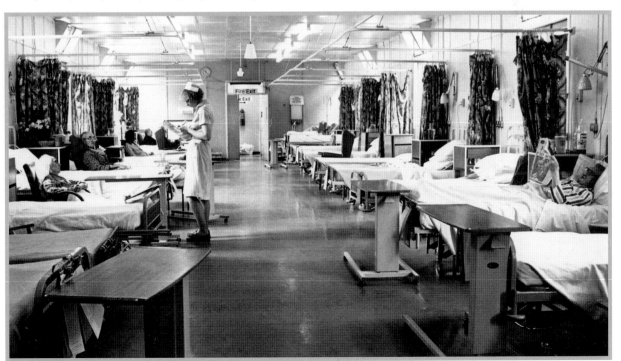

CAUTION
DO NOT TOUCH THE APPARATUS
IF TREATMENT FEELS MORE
THAN COMFORTABLY WARM CALL
FOR ASSISTANCE AT ONCE

Chesterfield Royal Hospital, Physiotherapy Department, April 1984.

Chesterfield Royal Hospital, Basil Ward, 1984.

The Alexander Nursing Home, Holywell Street, Durant Road. Formerly the Royal Hospital Nurses' Home.

Scarsdale Hospital during its demolition in 2000.

POLICE AND PUBLIC ORDER

The formation of an effective police force in the town did not really take place until the middle of the 19th century when the first day-time constables were appointed. At the beginning of the century the maintenance of law and order remained largely in the hands of the Manor Court, who appointed five constables to work under the direction of the magistrates. This state of affairs continued for some years and a report of 1829 stated: 'There is no paid police except that the Corporation gives a suit of clothes to one of the constables who acts as their servant, and generally another £20 to another as prison keeper. There are three other constables, who have only the fees of their office'. In addition there was also a night watch, which was maintained by public subscription.

This combination of five part-time untrained constables and a privately-supported night watch was clearly inadequate to deal with the problems of drunkenness, prostitution and general disorder which were beginning to afflict the town at this time. The situation began to improve after 1835 when the Municipal Corporations Act placed an obligation on each Corporation to appoint a watch committee. Within three weeks each watch committee was required to 'enrol a sufficient number of fit men who shall be sworn in before some Justice of the Peace, having jurisdiction within the borough to act as constables for preserving the peace by day and night, and preventing robberies and felonies and apprehending offenders against the peace'. At Chesterfield the Corporation acted swiftly. In January 1836 they decided to appoint seven men, superintended by an inspector, to provide a night watch. In 1839 the council also accepted responsibility for the fire service and appointed an engine keeper and three firemen.

There were, however, problems in recruiting and retaining reliable and sober individuals for the post of constable. Contemporary records contain several references to drunkenness and absenteeism, and by April 1836 six of the seven constables appointed in January had either resigned or been dismissed. Nor did this new police force seem to be very successful at maintaining the peace. Although the town was generally quiet during the week, serious disorder often prevailed on Saturday nights, and a report of 1832 described some streets in the town as 'literally teeming with drunken men and disorderly prostitutes'.

Later in the 1830s the presence of 'navvies' working on the Chesterfield Canal and the formation of Chartist groups in the area added to the threat of violent disorder. Generally the police coped well but on a number of occasions the military were drafted into the town to maintain the peace. The routine activities of the police at this time were, however, mainly concerned with the enforcement of by-laws introduced by the new Corporation in 1836. These included taking action against individuals who allowed animals to wander, emptied privies during the daytime or obstructed the streets.

A policeman on his beat on Old Road around 1910.

Chesterfield Fire Brigade at their Beetwell Street headquarters. The photograph shows the fire-fighting team with their new Merryweather fire engine. Also present is their older horse-drawn engine, which was first used in 1891.

For many years the police force was no more than a night watch, but in 1846 the decision was made to appoint two daytime policemen. Eight years later the town council also appointed four extra night-watchmen as a consequence of disturbances on Saturdays and Sundays, following the fortnightly payment of wages at coal and iron works just outside the borough. Attempts were also made to maintain high standards of behaviour and integrity within the force. In 1859 Superintendant Radford reported a sergeant and a constable to the watch committee for having received money for Christmas boxes. They were fined five shillings each and ordered to return the money. Two years later three constables were cautioned for playing dominoes in the Flying Horse beer house, despite the fact that they were off duty and claimed that they were not playing for money.

When Chesterfield extended its boundaries in 1892 the force comprised one head constable, one inspector, three sergeants and 12 constables. The final report made by the head constable to the old town council on 31 October 1892 reveals that although drunkenness and assault remained the most common offences, the police also spent a considerable amount of time rounding up stray animals and returning them to their owners. These included 50 sheep, 33 horses, seven pigs, five cows, two asses, two goats, two fowl and one rabbit! Following the extension of the borough the police force was increased in size, although its responsibilities remained the same.

The force continued to develop and evolve under the leadership of chief constables Emery (1882–1900) and Kilpatrick (1900–1923). By 1923 it had a complement of one chief constable, five inspectors (including a detective inspector and a chief clerk), five sergeants and 54 constables. Drunkenness, larceny, house breaking and burglary remained the most common offences that the force had to deal with during the inter-war period, but from time to time the police also had to deal with more serious crimes including the hijacking of a lorry and the attempted armed robbery of a sub-post office. The success of Chesterfield Town Football Club during this period resulted in increased attendances at the Saltergate Ground and the borough council authorised the purchase of two police horses to assist in crowd control. Other responsibilities of the Chesterfield force at this time included the enforcement of poor law legislation, the destruction of stray dogs and cats and the management of road traffic. To cater for the rapidly increasing number of cars driving into the centre of Chesterfield, the police designated seven car parks to the south of the Market Place. The Chesterfield force also pioneered the use of forensic science in its investigations, the introduction of daily occurrence reporting and the compilation of weekly crime bulletins. It was also a pioneer in its employment policies and in 1925 it appointed its first policewoman (Jessie Webster). The police force remained responsible for the fire service within the town and the *Chesterfield Yearbook and Directory* for 1920 noted that the fire brigade was well equipped with appliances for extinguishing fires, including a motor engine, a steam engine and an escape ladder. The chief constable acted as captain of the brigade and conveniently the fire station was located adjacent to the police station at the Municipal Hall.

Policeman on duty in Chesterfield town centre, c.1910.

Policemen on duty in West Bars in around 1910.

The outbreak of World War Two also had an impact on the work of the police. ARP duties, the enforcement of blackout regulations and various activities relating to civil defence were added to their existing responsibilities. By 1940 the strength of the force had been increased to a chief constable with two chief inspectors, 11 sergeants, 69 constables and one policewoman. In addition, a number of special constables had also been recruited.

The Chesterfield force retained its autonomy throughout World War Two but in 1947 it was amalgamated with the Derbyshire Constabulary. Today, Chesterfield and North Derbyshire is one of four divisions covering the county. Led by a chief superintendant, also known as the divisional commander, it covers Chesterfield, Clay Cross, Dronfield, Staveley and parts of the Bolsover District Council area. Its headquarters are at Chesterfield Police Station in Beetwell Street. The division is divided into three policing areas, of which Chesterfield is one. Also based at Chesterfield Police Station, this area is led by a senior inspector who is responsible for the policing of the town centre and the surrounding residential areas. In addition to the police station in Chesterfield, there is also another at Staveley as well as a mobile police station which visits residential areas on a regular basis. The force is committed to neighbourhood policing and dedicated teams of police officers work with partner agencies to focus upon resolving house burglaries and vehicle crimes. Together with criminal damage, these offences are responsible for a large proportion of the recorded crime on the Chesterfield Borough Policing Section.

The demonstration of new steam fire engine in the Market Place, c.1900.

Chesterfield's mounted police outside a police station (possibly Beetwell Street) in the 1920s.

A fire engine demonstration in the Market Place, c.1900.

A police parade, including a Ford Pilot and Fordson vans, 1920s.

Police officers assembled outside Beetwell Street police station in around 1940.

The VE Day Parade of special constables.

Staveley Police Force marching past the Nag's Head public house on Chesterfield Road.

Police and Fire Station at the junction of Tontine Road and Beetwell Street in the 1930s.

Derbyshire Constabulary traffic officers, based at Chesterfield division in the 1940s.

DCBM101099 – Image Courtesy of Derbyshire Police Collections (Buxton Museum and Art Gallery)

Special constable 256, Derby County and Borough police, working in the control room of Chesterfield Police Station in around 1968.

Police uniforms from the 1890s to the 1980s.

BEER AND SKITTLES – PUBLIC HOUSES AND BREWERIES IN CHESTERFIELD

The earliest inns and taverns were probably established in Chesterfield in the mediaeval period. They would have sold ale brewed on the premises and served from the barrel. In addition, many housewives would also have brewed their own ale. We do not know the names of these mediaeval alehouses but they were probably scattered between the church and the Market Place and possibly on the approaches to the town. Church ales were also brewed at this time to raise funds for the parish church. The earliest surviving pub in the town is the Royal Oak in The Shambles. Built on the site of a mediaeval building which may have served as a guest house of the Knights Templar, it was entirely rebuilt in 1748. It was then extensively restored in 1898 after the Batteson family sold it to William Stones Brewery.

The Royal Oak, The Shambles.

Celia Fiennes, who visited the town in 1697, commented that the town had 'the best ale in the kingdom'. The existence of four malthouses in the town may also indicate the presence of a number of inns at this time.

The Georgian era saw the development of a number of coaching inns within the town where horses could be changed and stabled, and food, drink and sometimes accommodation was provided for travellers. One of the most important of these was the Angel Inn (in the Market Place) but directories of the period also mention the Star Inn, the Old Angel and the Three Horse Shoes. These inns were also important commercial and social centres used for meetings, entertainment, sales, auctions and inquests.

During the 18th and 19th centuries a number of friendly societies were based in public houses. In 1797, for example, members of the society at the Nag's Head paid a monthly subscription of 1s as well as 2d for expenses. According to a survey published in the same year, 'Persons who have been registered members for two years are allowed weekly, in the case of sickness, 8s a week during one year; and if they continue ill a longer time, 5s a week during the remainder of their illness. From £2 to £5 are allowed towards the funeral of a member. A member, on the death of his wife, receives from each brother member 6d.'

The Angel Inn hosted winter assemblies. A poster dating from 1816 announced four assemblies for the period November 1816 to February 1817. The subscription for all four assemblies was 10s 6d and included tea and sandwiches. Dancing commenced at 9pm and would have provided an opportunity for the eligible bachelors to meet young ladies of the town.

The Angel Inn transformed itself into the Angel Hotel and continued to adapt to the times. A guide to the town published in 1899 stated that it had been 'brought completely up to date in its arrangements and appliances'. The public rooms included a coffee room, commercial room and a fine billiard room containing three excellent billiard tables. The hotel provided 20 bedrooms which were described as 'extremely comfortable and airy'. Many guests still arrived by horse and carriage, and another feature of the hotel was the stabling accommodation which provided for as many as 80 horses and a large number of vehicles.

The coming of the railways encouraged the building of a number of commercial hotels to cater for the needs of businessmen and travelling salesmen. These were usually located close to railway stations, and in Chesterfield the Station Hotel, Commercial Hotel and the Midland Hotel all fulfilled this function. The Station Hotel also catered for the growing popularity of cycling and proclaimed that every security was provided for cyclists' machines, with the town guide stating that 'tourists on wheels largely patronise the establishment during the season'.

The Angel Hotel, formerly the Angel Inn, High Street, 1902.

The Commercial Hotel, South Street, 1967.

The Station Hotel, Corporation Street, c.1899. Now the Chesterfield Hotel, the Station Hotel was built by the Chesterfield Brewery Company and opened in 1877.

Brampton Brewery, 1903.

The growth of the temperance movement was also reflected in the establishment of Freeman's Temperance Commercial Hotel in Corporation Street. Apart from being alcohol free it provided all the comforts of similar licensed premises, including 'handsomely furnished commercial and dining rooms, finely appointed billiard saloons, and 14 large, airy and comfortable bedrooms, provided with every modern requisite and convenience, bathroom, lavatory, etc.'

During the 19th and 20th centuries three breweries were producing a wide range of beers within the town. The first to be founded was the Brampton Brewery, which was established at a site between Chatsworth Road and Wheat Bridge sometime in the 1830s. This brewery produced a wide range of beers which varied over the years according to the fashion and taste of the time. An advertisement of 1892 lists Golden Bud and Derbyshire Extra Strong Ales, India Pale Ale, Double Stout and Family Pale Ale on draught as well as a range of bottled beers. The brewery owned around 100 pubs in Chesterfield as well as others further afield. The area covered by Brampton tied houses ranged from Sheffield in the north to Denby in the south, and from Mansfield in the east to Eyam in the west. Originally deliveries were made by horse-drawn dray. The horses were stabled at the brewery during the week but at weekends were taken to a field behind the Terminus Hotel for a well-earned rest.

The early years of the 20th century were a period of growth and expansion. Existing tied houses were rebuilt or drastically improved, more pubs were purchased and sales to free houses were increased. The success of the company, however, led to its takeover by Warwick's and Richardson's in 1955. Production ceased in the same year and today the site is occupied by a large B&Q store. The Chesterfield Brewery commenced production in 1854. It produced a wide range of beers and won awards at the Brewers' Exhibition in London in 1911, 1914 and 1918. Encouraged by these successes, the company embarked on a major programme of pub rebuilding and renovation. This, however, placed a severe strain on the company's finances and it closed in 1935 following a takeover by the Mansfield Brewery Company. The Scarsdale Brewery was the smallest of the Chesterfield breweries. Never more than a small family concern, it nevertheless gained a reputation for the quality of its products and won many prizes for its beers and stouts. It was taken over by Whitbread's in 1958 and in the following year brewing ceased.

Drunkenness proved to be something of a problem in the town during the 1920s and 1930s, particularly on Friday and Saturday nights, and the issue was exported to outlying areas (particularly Staveley) where many of the public houses had been granted music licenses. World War Two brought shortages of both beer and glasses. This, together with blackout regulations and the call-up of thousands of young men, may have resulted in a reduction in problems of drunkenness in the area.

The second half of the 20th century saw major changes in the ownership of local pubs as well as the development of 'fun pubs' and theme pubs. There has also been an increased focus on the sale of meals at pubs. The most recent trend in the brewing industry has been the development of micro-breweries. Chesterfield's contribution to this development is the Spire Brewery at Staveley. Established by David McLaren in 2006, this small local brewery produces nine regular beers as well as a number of seasonal specials. It has won a number of awards for its beers and goes from strength to strength. In August 2007 it acquired its first pub; the Britannia on Ward Street, New Tupton. The people of Chesterfield continue to enjoy good-quality beer in convivial surroundings.

STONES
CANNON
ALES

The Royal Oak Public House, The Shambles, 1952. It is said to be the oldest building in the town, with parts dating back to the 16th century. The pub was purchased by William Stone Brewery from the Bateson family in 1897 and underwent extensive renovation.

Restoration work being carried out on the Royal Oak in 1898.

The Shambles and Royal Oak Public House, c.1910.

The Royal Oak, c.1910. The photograph shows the pub's urinals on the far right. The urinals were later demolished and a barber's shop built on the site.

The Old Ship Inn, St Mary's Gate, 1882. The Old Ship was demolished in 1887.

The Victoria Inn, Brampton. The Victoria Inn was built around 1860 by Samuel Hoskin, who sold it to Ind Coope Brewery in 1886. Punch Taverns took it over in 2003.

The Square and Compass Public House, West Bars, 1910.

The Terminus Hotel and Restaurant, c.1900–10. Built on the site of the Old Pheasant Inn, it was so named because it was the end of the line for the electric tram from Low Pavement.

The Old Pheasant Inn, Chatsworth Road, Brampton, c.1902.

Coach and horses outside the Yellow Lion Public House, Saltergate, c.1900.

The Blue Bell Inn, Cavendish Street. The photograph was taken in the late 1930s when the inn was newly built.

A club outing from the Devonshire Arms, Staveley, 1940s.

The Out of Town Public House, Goytside, Brampton, 1991. This was formerly the Furnace Inn.

Ye Old Crooked Spire Public House, 1985. Now the Slug and Fiddle.

St George's Works, Knifesmithgate, c.1900. This was a soda water bottling factory and store for T.P. Wood's wine and spirit business, established in 1862. Shortly before Wood's death in 1911 the business was bought by the Chesterfield Brewery Company and later by Mansfield Brewery.

Brampton Brewery. The Brampton Brewery was situated between Chatsworth Road and Wheatbridge Road where the B&Q store now stands. The building was demolished in 1984.

FRESH AIR AND FUN – PARKS AND PUBLIC SPACES IN CHESTERFIELD

The first public park to be established in Chesterfield was Queen's Park. This was created in 1887 to commemorate the jubilee of Queen Victoria. On 21 September of that year a 'monster procession' made its way through the town to the new park. The Sherwood Rangers provided a cavalry escort for the five carriages carrying the members of the jubilee committee, and the 24 drays represented the major trades of the town. These were also accompanied by large numbers of school children and members of local societies. A service of dedication was held and a commemorative tree planted to mark the event. In 1890 an adjacent five-acre field was purchased and when the park was formally opened in 1893 it comprised a general recreation area as well as a lake, cricket ground, children's playground and a bandstand. The first glass houses were constructed in the park in 1897. They were used to propagate plants for use in a number of parks within the borough.

As the largest public open space in the town, Queen's Park was used to commemorate important events in the life of the nation. These included the relief of Mafeking during the Boer War, the coronation of King Edward VII and celebrations to mark the end of World War One. Later in the century the park was the site of celebrations organised by the borough council to commemorate the silver jubilee of George V and the coronation of George VI.

The park provided facilities for a wide range of sports and leisure activities. The most significant of these was cricket. From the outset the cricket ground was laid out to a high standard with the intention that county sides might play there. Chesterfield Cricket Club moved there and the first county cricket match was held in 1898. Derbyshire County Cricket Club regularly played some of its matches there from 1898 until 1998, returning in 2006. Large crowds came to watch these matches, particularly during the 1930s when during three seasons the county club chose to have its most attractive fixture, against the Australian touring side, played at Queen's Park.

Other clubs and organisations made extensive use of the facilities within the park. Various amateur football clubs played their matches on a Saturday; although for many years the Corporation refused to allow Sunday games. Athletics and cycling events were also staged in the park from the earliest years of its existence, and later facilities for tennis, bowls and 'pitch and put' were added.

The annual flower show of the Chesterfield and District Horticultural Society was held here from 1893 until 1934, when it made significant losses. These were popular events attracting large crowds. Local newspaper accounts paint a vivid picture of some of the early shows when, in addition to the various classes for fruit and vegetables, there were also athletics and cycling events, music and fireworks. On a few occasions the visitors were also entertained by a balloon ascent!

Queen's Park and lake, c.1900s.

Bandstand, Queen's Park, Chesterfield, 1978. This is the third bandstand, which was built in 1922 to replace an original wooden structure which was demolished in 1919. The temporary second bandstand was moved to Bradley Park.

The lake has always been an important and popular feature of the park. Rowing boats have been available for hire since 1894 and a motor boat was purchased in 1936. It was named the *Queen Mary* and in the first season of operation a trip round the lake cost 2d for adults and 1d for children. The lake was also used for sailing model boats and in the winter when it froze it became an unofficial skating rink.

Brass band concerts were a popular feature in the summer months, and for many years concerts were held every Sunday and on most Wednesdays and some bank holidays. In the 1950s dance bands were hired to provide entertainment at Whitsun and August bank holidays. A decade later these were succeeded by local pop groups.

World War Two brought changes to the way in which the park was used. The Annexe was requisitioned by the military authorities as a drill ground and later for accommodation. Some facilities remained available to the public but had to be shared with the military. The park was also used as part of the Holidays at Home scheme in which a wide range of activities were organised for adults and children. Iodine tablets were hung from the trees and these, together with donkey rides, swing boats and roundabouts, created something of the magic of a seaside holiday!

The immediate post-war period saw the beginning of a decline in the park's fortunes. For a number of reasons fewer large-scale events were held there. The creation of the National Health Service meant that there was no longer a need for fundraising events for the hospital. In addition, an increasing numbers of families began to take their holidays at the seaside; although the council continued to organise a 'Summer Entertainments Programme'. Cricket, athletics and brass band concerts continued to attract large numbers of people on a regular basis, although budget cuts in the late 1950s meant that some of the 'big name' bands no longer visited the park.

Other significant changes and improvements were made to the park in the second half of the 20th century. In 1967 the children's playground was moved to make way for a swimming pool and in 1976 a miniature railway was constructed. In 1987 the Queen's Park Leisure Centre was opened, providing a wide range of sporting and leisure facilities including a heated swimming pool. Following the award of a grant from the Heritage lottery Fund in 2003, Queen's Park was renovated and improved and many of its old historic features restored.

Queen's Park, however, was not the only important open area within the town. In the early years of the 20th century Alderman G.A. Eastwood presented Eastwood Park to the people of Hasland, while Brearley Park was established in the Whittington area. At Brampton, Pearson's Recreation Ground was created on land donated to Chesterfield Corporation in May 1913 by Mrs Helen Pearson, in memory of her late husband, Alderman James Pearson. The iron railings and entrance gates were provided by Mr C.P. Markham, and the ground was fully laid out and in use by the following year.

During the inter-war years Pearson's Recreation Ground was widely used by a number of local amateur football clubs including Brampton Athletic FC, Brampton Rangers, Brampton United and Brampton Gospel Mission FC. Following the war a new pitch was laid out to FA specifications and let to Brampton Rovers, who played there for several years before moving to another ground.

From the 1940s the Recreation Ground was also visited regularly by travelling fairs and circuses, including Paulo's Royal Circus, Reco Brothers' Empire Circus and Robert Fossett's London Circus & Zoo. An advertisement for a visit by Paulo's Royal Circus in 1943 announced performances by 'ponderous elephants, riders, acrobats, monkeys, dogs, pigeons, wire walkers, dancing horses, midget ponies, equestrians, oriental mysteries, a host of clowns, etc, etc.' Tickets cost four shillings and the big top provided seating for 2,000 people. Such entertainment became less popular in the 1960s and the last visit by a

Queen's Park Café.

The opening ceremony of Eastwood Park.

The Village Concert Hall in Eastwood Park, c.1935.

circus came in 1966, when Robert Fossett and George Sanger's Combined Circus featured TV personality Mr Pastry (Richard Hearn) as their star act.

As the town expanded, other parks and play areas were created either by the Corporation or through the generosity of local benefactors. In 1927, for example, Robinson's donated a large area of land along the upper stretches of the Hipper to create the Somersall Playing Fields. Elsewhere in the borough, open spaces and children's play areas were created as part of new housing developments.

In recent years the reclamation of derelict colliery sites has provided opportunities for creating leisure facilities. At Staveley the site of the former Ireland Colliery has been transformed into the Poolsbrook Country Park. Developed jointly by Derbyshire County Council and Chesterfield Borough Council, this 180-acre park has become an important leisure amenity enjoyed by large numbers of local people. In addition to large areas of woodland and grassland, the park also contains 23 acres of green water. This has been designed to attract wild birds, and ornithologists have observed a wide range of species, including Great Crested Grebe, Cormorants, Mute Swans, Wheatears and Yellow Wagtails.

The Park is designed to attract a wide range of visitors and also contains a children's adventure play area, picnic sites, sledging slopes and lakes for anglers. There are also trails for walkers, cyclists and horse riders. In 2006 a Community Café was established in the visitor centre and volunteers now provide a range of drinks and snacks for visitors at weekends and bank holidays throughout the year.

Today, Chesterfield Borough Council is responsible for 46 parks and open spaces, covering 689 acres in total. According to its own website, the council also provides 41 football pitches, seven cricket pitches, seven bowling greens, one athletics track, six tennis courts, two golf courses, 69 children's play areas, one boating lake and four course fishing venues. It seems that in the 21st century the people of Chesterfield have plenty of opportunities for fresh air and fun!

The mayor and town council at the dedication of Queen's Park in September 1887.

The trade dray of Hinch's Shoeing Forge decorated for the procession at the dedication of Queen's Park in September 1887.

The trade dray of Joseph Clayton, tanners, decorated for the procession at the dedication of Queen's Park, September 1887.

Queen's Park in 1910.

Queen's Park lake in 1910.

Queen's Park bandstand, 1900s.

Queen's Park childrens' play area.

Queen's Park showing leisure centre and miniature railway.

Queen's Park conservatory.

Empire Day celebrations in Queen's Park, 1913.

Chesterfield Agricultural Show held on the Recreation Ground, Saltergate, c.1910.

Spectators at Chesterfield Flower Show, c.1900s.

The Concert Hall in Eastwood Park, Hasland, c.1950s. The fountain in the foreground was moved to Chesterfield's New Square in the early 1980s but was later removed and returned.

Alpine Gardens, c.1910. The Alpine Gardens were presented to the town by Alderman T.P. Wood in 1909. They were removed in 1932 to make way for a new road, Church Way, linking Burlington Street with St Mary's Gate.

PLAYING THE GAME – AMATEUR AND PROFESSIONAL SPORT IN CHESTERFIELD

Chesterfield has a long history of involvement in amateur and professional sport. The first recorded game of cricket in Derbyshire took place in September 1757 when Sheffield Cricket Club played a match against Wirksworth at Brampton Moor, near Chesterfield. Chesterfield Cricket Club was founded some years later and played its matches at various locations in the town including the recreation ground on Saltergate. In February 1894, however, the club obtained the use of the new cricket ground on Queen's Park. The club played its first game there on 5 May of the same year and two years later won its first Derbyshire League title. In 1899 an impressive new pavilion (still in use today) was built at a cost of £499 18s 6d. Although it achieved some success in the first half of the century, the 'golden years' of the club were between 1947 and 1957 when the first XI won the Derbyshire League title six times in 10 seasons. Following this period of success the club joined the Bassetlaw League, where it played for the next 41 years. In 1999 the club joined the Derbyshire Premier League, in which it continues to play.

Derbyshire County Cricket Club has also played county matches at Chesterfield for over a century. Founded in 1870, the club played at least two matches at the Saltergate ground before playing for the first time at Queen's Park in 1898. The famous cricketer W.G. Grace played here on two occasions, in 1901 and 1904. County cricket was played here until 1998 and returned in 2006 with a County Championship game against Worcester and a One Day League game against Surrey. Queen's Park remains a popular venue and it is anticipated that the county side will continue to play some of its matches there.

Chesterfield Football Club was founded in 1867 when the Chesterfield Cricket Club advertised for members to play during the winter months. This club collapsed in 1881 but two other clubs (both known as Chesterfield Town FC) played in the Football League between 1884 and 1917. The present Chesterfield FC was formed as Chesterfield Municipal Football Club in 1919. Chesterfield have spent most of their history in the lower divisions of the Football League. The team enjoyed mixed fortunes for many years but were promoted to Division Three in 1985. Further success came in the 1995 when they won the Division Three Play-off Final at Wembley and were promoted to the Second Division. Two years later they reached the semi-final of the FA Cup. The club finished eighth in the Second Division in the 2007–08 season. Throughout its history the club has played at the Saltergate Ground but plans are in place for the building of a new stadium on the former Dema Glass site. Planning permission has been received and at the time of writing it is still hoped that the new stadium will be opened in 2010.

Chesterfield Races and Funfair.

Chesterfield Market Place. Unloading pheasants from the King's shoot at Chatsworth.

Advert for Service Motors, 1920. The company catered for the growing popularity of motor sport.

Football and cricket are not the only spectator sports which are popular in Chesterfield. For over two centuries the town also hosted the 'sport of kings'. Chesterfield Races date from the time of the 1st Duke of Devonshire, who donated land for a racecourse on Newbold Common, as it was then called. The track was two miles long and enclosed most of Whittington Moor. For a number of years it attracted members of the aristocracy and in the 1840s Lord Chesterfield was a regular and popular entrant. By the 1920s attendances ranged from 10,000 to 50,000. The last race meeting was held in July 1929, and the land was later used for housing.

Field sports were also popular with the nobility and the gentry. Shooting was particularly popular on the moors around the town and the King regularly visited nearby Chatsworth to shoot pheasant.

Bowls have been played in Chesterfield since at least the 17th century and probably much earlier. The Corporation acquired the land on which the bowling green was located in 1604 and there is documentary evidence that in 1664 Sir George Sitwell adjourned the sittings of the Chesterfield Quarter Sessions in order to play bowls with friends on the green. It remained a popular sport for several centuries and by the early years of the 20th there were a number of bowling greens in the town, including those at the Portland, Terminus and Britannia hotels.

A range of other sports have also provided entertainment and exercise for local people over the years. At various times organisations and clubs have been established for the promotion and enjoyment of a wide range of activities. In 1903 the town possessed an angling association, a cycling club, a chess club, a golf club, a homing pigeon society and a ping pong club. The programme of the 1914 Shopping Festival also recorded that facilities for tennis, rollerskating and boxing were available in the town. Swimming was also a popular pastime at this time. The Chesterfield Swimming Club made use of an enclosed

A cartoon from the The Link, *1919, depicting a match between Wheatbridge and Walton.*

pool at the Central Schools as well as an open-air pool at Inkerman. The club, which was organised into ladies' and gentlemen's sections, also organised an annual water carnival and aquatic sports at Walton Dam. Later, open air swimming pools were also established at Stand Road, Chatsworth Road (Markham Baths) and Ringwood Park. Motor sport became popular too in the early years of the 20th century and two clubs, the Chesterfield Motorcycle Club and the North Derbyshire Motor Cycle Club, came into existence before 1914.

Golf has also been popular in the town for many years. The Tapton Municipal Golf Course was opened in 1934 when a round of golf cost one shilling. The private Chesterfield Golf Club has a much longer history dating back to 1897, when its first members played on Somersall Park. The club moved to its present site at Walton in 1906. The original nine-hole course was extended in the 1920s but during World War Two some of the land was requisitioned and members were restricted to playing on just nine holes. Despite these restrictions in 1942 the famous Henry Cotton played an exhibition game against three local professionals to raise money for the Red Cross. At the end of the war the club received its land back, together with £338 3s 0d in compensation. In succeeding years improvements were made to both the course and the clubhouse and today the club provides excellent sporting and social facilities for its members. The Tapton Park Club also continues to flourish with a total membership of around 400, including a ladies' section and a junior section, which numbers just over a hundred.

For many years collieries and engineering firms promoted or supported football and cricket teams for their workers. Robinson's, as the largest employer in the town, provided facilities for football, cricket, hockey, bowls, tennis and swimming. It had extensive playing fields and a sports pavilion at Walton Mill Dam, and its bowling green was considered to be one of the finest in the area. Some pubs in the area also sponsored teams and, of course, most young people gained their first experience of competitive sport at school.

Today Chesterfield provides an extensive range of sporting facilities, and a wide variety of amateur organisations offer opportunities for local people of all ages to participate in a diverse range of sporting activities. A number of amateur football clubs play in local leagues with varying degrees of success, and in the summer cricket and tennis are played by large numbers of people in the local parks. The borough council provides facilities for football, cricket, rugby, tennis and golf. The Queen's Park Leisure Centre, opened in 1987, has an indoor swimming pool, a fitness centre and a number of indoor courts which can be used for a variety of sports. At Staveley the recently opened Healthy Living Centre has a 150-station gym, two dance studios, a health spa, 25-metre swimming pool, climbing wall and pirate-themed soft play area for children. The borough council works closely with schools and youth groups and the next generation of young people are being encouraged to keep fit and 'play the game'!

Queen's Park Leisure Centre, 2009.

The Healthy Living Centre, Staveley.

Dick Cushlow played football for Chesterfield from 1946–47.

Arthur Cox was manager of Chesterfield FC from 1976–80. He was also manager of Derby County FC from 1984 to 1993.

Steve Baines played for Chesterfield FC from 1983–86, playing in 154 games before leaving to join Matlock Town.

John Duncan was manager of Chesterfield FC from 1983 to 1987.

Mowing the Holmewood Colliery Cricket Club pitch with a pit pony, c.1930.

The Bowling Green outside the Municipal Hall, c.1956.

The Bowling Green, New Beetwell Street. The photograph shows the Bowling Green and Municipal Hall. The lower section of the hall with two arches housed the club's facilities. The Municipal Hall was erected after the old Guild Hall was demolished in 1847.

Chesterfield Bowling Green, Beetwell Street. The photograph shows club members in 1911.

A swimming sports day at Walton Dam, c.1905.

A swimming sports day at Walton Dam, 1931.

Ringwood Swimming Pool in the 1930s.

Sports Meeting at Queen's Park, c.1960s.

Netherthorpe Grammar School girls' hockey team, c.1925.

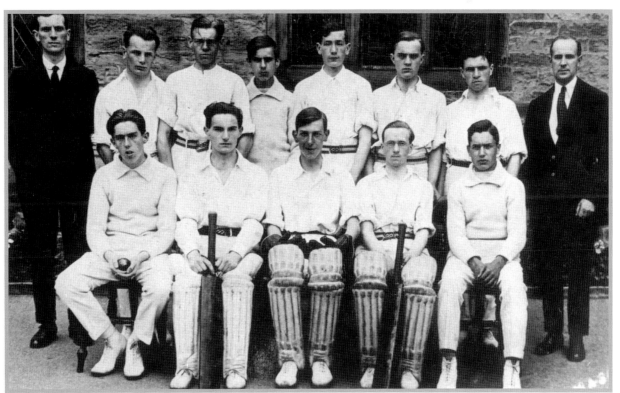

Netherthorpe Grammar School boys' cricket team, c.1930s.

Sports Day at Chesterfield Grammar School, c.1910.

Brimington Boys' School football team of the 1906–07 season posing with their trophy.

The Hollingwood gymnastics team practising outside the Staveley company offices, c.1930.

Chesterfield Wheelers Cycle Club, which ran between 1920s–30s.

Middlecroft Leisure Centre, 1988.

Stand Road Racecourse, Whittington Moor, c.1910.

Chesterfield Races – The finishing post, judges' box and 'new' stand, photographed in the early 1920s.

Chesterfield Races and Funfair, early 1920s.

FOOTLIGHTS AND FLEA PITS — THEATRE AND CINEMA ENTERTAINMENT IN CHESTERFIELD

Plays and other forms of entertainment were probably performed at inn yards during the Tudor period and perhaps even earlier. There are references to bear baiting and bull baiting in the town dating from the Middle Ages, and it seems likely that entertainers as well as pedlars would have visited the town during the annual fairs. The street name 'Glumangate' may refer to the gleemen or minstrels who lived there. Others have suggested that it was in this area that minstrels performed on market days or during fairs.

The first theatre in Chesterfield, the Theatre Royal, was established in the 17th century and came into the hands of the Corporation around 1620. Situated in Theatre Yard, for many years it offered a range of plays including comedies, dramas and Shakespearean works. There was no single repertory company based in Chesterfield at this time but the theatre was leased to a variety of actor managers for varying periods. Some returned to the town on a number of occasions and the *Derby Mercury* of 22 September 1830 reported 'our old friend Mr Manley opened the Chesterfield Theatre on Monday last, when for the first time it was to be illuminated with gas. Several new performers have been added to the company since their last visit, and the spirited efforts of the manager to contribute to the amusement of the public will, we hope, be crowned with equal success to his efforts'. For many years this traditional theatre, complete with dress circle, gallery and pit, was often thronged with playgoers. In 1839 the Revd George Hall in his *History of Chesterfield* wrote: 'The theatre, which is a plain brick building, in a yard at the bottom of the Market Place, is rented by Mr Manley and is the property of the Corporation. The interior of the building is neat, and some years ago was crowded every

An advertisement for the Hippodrome from 1917.

Stephenson's Memorial Hall.

Proctor's Bioscope sideshow at the Chesterfield Races, around 1909.

DCCC001571 – Courtesy of C H Nadin, Photographer

Corporation Theatre,

CHESTERFIELD.

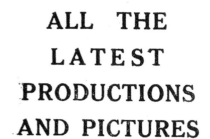

ALL THE
LATEST
PRODUCTIONS
AND PICTURES

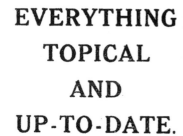

EVERYTHING
TOPICAL
AND
UP-TO-DATE.

Popular Prices.

HIPPODROME

Corporation Street, Chesterfield.

THE HOME OF
. UP-TO-DATE .
VARIETY SHOWS

Two Houses Nightly.

An advertisement from 1920 for the Corporation Theatre and the Hippodrome.

night during the season with the gentry of the town and neighbourhood.' But he also noted that 'A very visible falling-off has taken place in the drama during the last few years – whether from a change of habit or education, or from the altered state of the times, it is not our province to inquire'.

Perhaps partly because of this decline the theatre was also used by a variety of groups for concerts and fundraising activities. In September 1855, for example, the *Morning Chronicle* reported that 'a dramatic performance was given in the Chesterfield Theatre…by the officers of the Chatsworth Rifles in aid of the Crimean Fund'. Following its closure, the building was used for a number of years as the town's fire station.

A new Theatre Royal was established in Corporation Street in 1886. This was taken over by Chesterfield Hippodromes Ltd in 1912 and renamed as the Hippodrome. A wide range of variety artistes performed here, including 'Chung Ling Soo, the famous Chinese conjurer and illusionist; Vasco; the extraordinarily gifted "Mad Musician" Fred Karno's companies; and other headliners'. These star acts were supported by comedians, vocalists, acrobats and other speciality acts.

But the Theatre Royal was not the only playhouse in the town. The Corporation Theatre, housed within Stephenson's Memorial Hall, was opened in 1879. Travelling companies performed plays and other entertainments here and in the early years of the 20th century the Corporation spent a considerable amount in raking the floor, improving the heating and other minor works. This, too, was primarily a variety theatre and during the town's shopping festival in 1914 the official souvenir booklet noted that, 'the programme will include a strong "David Garrick" sketch and Darcy's company in a musical scene, and, for the second week, the Aeroplane Ladies and their sensational act, and the Comic Eltons will be prominent turns'.

The Hippodrome Theatre in 1956. The Hippodrome opened in 1886 as the Theatre Royal. It reopened in 1912 as the Hippodrome and closed in 1954. It was later demolished.

By the start of the 20th century theatres began to be challenged by the new picture houses or cinemas. The first moving pictures were shown in travelling bioscope booths at travelling fairs. Photographs taken in the early years of the 20th century at the Chesterfield Races and fair show people queuing to watch a bioscope show. The Theatre Royal also began to show silent films in the early years of the 20th century. At first these were just short films lasting a few minutes and were part of a more general Vaudeville programme. By 1908, however, some whole weeks were devoted to film shows provided by organisations such as the Great London Animated Picture Co. The theatre had only one projector at this time, however, and variety acts were still used to keep the audience entertained while reels were changed. By January 1913 films were being regularly advertised as 'the latest pictures on the bioscope'.

In 1930 sound equipment was installed and in September of that year audiences were able to watch their first talking picture: *The Hollywood Revue* starring Jack Benny, Buster Keaton and Joan Crawford. This was not the first talking picture to be shown in Chesterfield, for the Victoria (later the Gaumont) was able to show *The Singing Fool* starring Al Jolson as early as July 1929. In less than a decade, however, the Hippodrome had been leased to Terrance Byrom Ltd and reverted to live entertainment. These live shows continued throughout the war years. The theatre struggled on into the 1950s but finally closed its doors for the last time in 1954.

The Regal Club, Church Street, Staveley. This photograph was taken in 1988. The building used to be the Regal Cinema but was later converted into the Regal Bingo and Social Club. It has since closed.

Advertising poster for the Empire, Staveley, 1915.

Other cinemas, however, provided film entertainment throughout the first half of the 20th century. In 1907 the Brampton Coliseum became the first building to be converted specifically for cinematic use. It had a chequered history but its inability to show the latest films on their release contributed to its downfall and it closed in 1957. Other early cinemas which survived until the 1950s and 1960s included the Lyceum in Whittington Moor, the Carlton in Hasland and the Regal in Staveley.

In Chesterfield the Picture House (later the Odeon), the ABC/Regal and the Gaumont entertained generations of cinemagoers throughout the greater part of the 20th century. They had to adapt to changing trends and new technology including 3D films, cinemascope and stereoscopic sound. The Gaumont survived until 1965, when it was converted into a Bingo Club. Later this was demolished to make way for the Victoria Centre, though the original façade remains.

The growth of the DVD market and the development of digital television led to a further decline in cinema going in the latter years of the 20th century. In Chesterfield, the Odeon became the Winding Wheel conference centre and the ABC/Canon in Cavendish Street finally closed down in 1991. The closure of older cinemas was, however, balanced by the opening of plush new multi-screen entertainment centres. This trend was reflected in Chesterfield in the 1990s when a Cineworld multiplex cinema was opened within the Alma Leisure complex just off the Derby Road roundabout. Today the latest films are shown on 10 screens. Movie fans in Chesterfield have never had so much choice!

But amateur and professional theatre still thrives in Chesterfield. The Pomegranate Theatre was opened by the actress Kathleen Harrison on 19 February 1949. Stars who appeared there early in their career include Donald Sutherland, Nigel Davenport and David McCallum. Previously known as the Civic Theatre, it changed its name to the Pomegranate in 1982. Today its programme includes a range of plays and musicals performed by local amateur groups and professional touring companies, and people come from as far afield as Derby to enjoy the productions. The Pomegranate Theatre celebrated its 60th anniversary in 2009 with a range of special activities including a gala evening and a programme which encompassed musicals, thrillers, comedies and ballet.

The Odeon Cinema after its closure. This photograph was taken in October 1986. The building is now used as the Winding Wheel Conference Centre.

From Turnpikes to Trains – Improvements in Transport in the Chesterfield Area

From at least the 16th century packhorse carriers and wagons had transported goods to and from Chesterfield. The growth of trade and industry in the 18th century, however, led to the need for an improvement in transport. The first improvement was the construction of turnpike roads. Turnpike roads had to be authorised by an Act of Parliament which empowered trusts or companies to build new roads or maintain existing highways. In return they were allowed to charge a toll to all those who used the road.

These improved roads led to an increase in the speed and frequency of traffic, and before long a new generation of stagecoaches travelling at speeds of up to 12 miles an hour were bringing ideas, fashions and news of great events to the town. The road from Sheffield and Chesterfield to Derby was turnpiked in 1756 and before long a complex network of routes provided a regular service between Chesterfield and other major towns and cities. Pigot's Directory of 1828 records the following coach services operating from the town:

'To LONDON, the Mail (from Leeds) calls at the Star Inn, New Square every morning at half-past two o'clock; goes thro' Nottingham, Melton, Kettering, Bedford, &c – the Comet (from Leeds) every afternoon at two o'clock; goes thro' Nottingham, Loughborough, Leicester, Northampton, &c. – the Comet (from Leeds) every afternoon at six, the same

route – the Hope (from Leeds) calls at the Angel Inn every morning at ten; goes thro' Nottingham, Melton, Kettering &c and the Courier (from Leeds) calls at the Old Angel, Packer's Row every morning at a quarter past seven; goes thro' Nottingham, Leicester, Northampton, &c.

To BIRMINGHAM, the Mail (from Sheffield) calls at the Star Inn, New Square, every morning at eight o' clock; goes thro' Derby, Burton & Litchfield – & the Amity (from Leeds) calls at the Old Angle, Packer's Row, every morning at a quarter past seven, goes the same route.

To LEEDS, the Mail (from London) calls at the Star Inn, New Square every afternoon at two o'clock; goes thro' Dronfield, Sheffield, Barnsley and Wakefield – the Express (from London) every day at twelve – the Courier (from London) calls at the Old Angel, Packer's Row, every day at half-past twelve – and then Amity (from Birmingham) at half-past two every afternoon.

To MANCHESTER, the Champion (from Nottingham) calls at then Angel Inn, New Square, every morning at ten o'clock; goes thro' Stoney Middleton, Chapel-en-le-Frith, Disley and Stockport, and at one o'clock every day; goes thro' Mansfield & Nottingham.

To SHEFFIELD, the Mail (from Birmingham) calls at the Star Inn, New Square every afternoon at a quarter before two o' clock; goes thro' Dronfield &c – and the Accommodation, from the Three Horse Shoes, High Street, every morning at eight.'

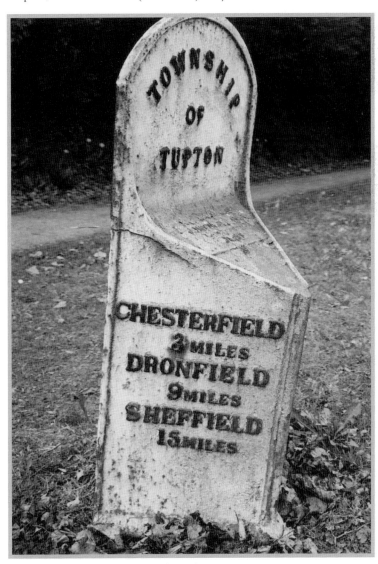

A milepost on the Chesterfield to Derby road.

A mail coach.

James Brindley.

Although the construction of turnpike roads did much to improve the speed and efficiency of road transport to and from towns such as Chesterfield, there was no integrated national system of roads and the transportation of heavy or bulky goods remained extremely expensive. Eventually, stage coaches and wagons were replaced by canals and railways.

The Chesterfield Canal was promoted by a number of interests, including the Cavendish family, who owned a furnace and forge at Staveley; the London Lead Company, who wanted a more convenient shipping place than Bawtry for the products of their smelting mill at Ashover; and several local landowners who wished to exploit their coal resources. James Brindley was engaged to make a survey and prepare plans and estimates. It was agreed that the route of the canal should run from Chesterfield to Northwood, past Shireoakes and Worksop to East Retford and thence to the River Trent at West Stockwith. An Act of Parliament authorising construction of the canal received the Royal Assent on 28 March 1771. When the news reached Chesterfield bells were rung in the churches and fireworks were let off in the Market Place. The canal took six years to build but was finally opened on 4 June 1777 with considerable ceremony and rejoicing. The *Derby Mercury* reported the arrival of the first boat from Stockwith in the following terms:

'The boat was met at the first lock by several gentlemen of the committee and a great number of proprietors, attended by a very large concourse of people, and was introduced with colours flying, the firing of guns and a band of music, after which the

The lock house on the Chesterfield Canal at Killamarsh, c.1900–10.

goods were unloaded and put into wagons, which were drawn to the town by the navigators, proceeded by the gentlemen of the committee and the proprietors, who walked in procession with the music playing before them. The assiduity of the workmen, whose labour for the last three weeks almost exceeds belief, was rewarded by a handsome treat given them by the proprietors, of which near 300 of them partook, and the gentlemen of the town concluded the day over a cheerful glass; the ringing of the bells, bonfires and fireworks contributing to the festivity of the evening.'

Traffic was slow to develop but increased considerably after the construction of horse-drawn tramways to collieries at Inkersall, Spinkhill, Norbriggs and Glasshouse Common. In 1789 the traffic on the canal comprised 42,000 tons of coal, 7,569 tons of stone, 4,366 tons of corn, 3,955 tons of lime, 3,862 tons of lead and 1,544 tons of iron together with smaller quantities of pottery, ale and other sundry items. Tonnage reached its peak in 1848, but by this time the canal had already been taken over by the Manchester, Sheffield and Lincolnshire Railway.

The coming of the railways was largely the cause of the decline of the canal system. The first railway to reach Chesterfield was the North Midland Railway, which arrived in Chesterfield in 1840. Engineered by George Stephenson and his assistant Frederick Swanwick, the line ran from Derby to Leeds, and, following a route along the valley of the River Rother, it passed through both Chesterfield and Staveley. The whole line from Leeds to Derby was opened on 1 July 1841 when a train of 43

George Stephenson, the railway pioneer.

147

The original North Midland Railway Station, c.1840. Chesterfield's first railway station opened as part of the North Midland Railway between Derby and Leeds in 1840. Built in the Tudor-style, the architect was Francis Thompson.

carriages pulled by two locomotives was greeted by a band when it stopped at Chesterfield Railway Station. Before long the extension of the railway network provided Chesterfield with a direct main line to London, Bristol, Edinburgh and Glasgow. It was not until 1893 that a second line reached the town. This was constructed by the Manchester, Sheffield and Lincolnshire Railway, who built a loop into the town. By 1898 this line provided the town with a second link to the capital via Nottingham, a route which closed to passengers in 1963. In 1897 the Lancashire, Derbyshire and East Counties Railway opened a station at Chesterfield Market Place. This line served the important coal-mining area of the Dukeries in Nottinghamshire and provided passengers with a service between Chesterfield and Lincoln.

During the Victorian period the railways had a huge impact on the lives of the people of Chesterfield. They brought national newspapers, fresh milk and produce to the town and provided 'paddy mails' to take miners from Chesterfield to work in coal mines outside the town. Railways also allowed local workers to take holidays in different parts of the country. The Midland Railway issued tourist tickets from Chesterfield to seaside resorts such as Morecambe, Blackpool, Cleethorpes, Sheringham, Cromer and Great Yarmouth.

The railways also created additional employment opportunities. Three wagon works were established on the outskirts of the town to manufacture, maintain and repair railway wagons. Other engineering companies also benefitted and, of course, the demand for coal increased.

Amalgamations, two world wars and nationalisation all had an impact on the railway services to and from Chesterfield. This, together in the growth of car ownership, led to the relative demise of the railway. Today the town has only one railway station, which was rebuilt only a few years ago. From here regular services are provided by a number of train companies to destinations throughout the country.

The Chesterfield Canal building. Looking towards Brimington Road, Chesterfield, 1908.

Chesterfield Canal at Killamarsh showing the entrance to the Norwood Tunnel. This was the second-largest tunnel in the country at the time of its construction in the 1770s. It collapsed in 1907.

A lock keepers' house/office on the Chesterfield Canal at Wharf Lane, Stonegravels, c.1890–1900.

Corporation Lock on the Chesterfield Canal, Retford, 1968.

The original Midland Railway Station, c.1868. The station had canopies added c.1860 but was demolished around 1875 to be replaced by a larger building.

The Manchester, Sheffield and Lincolnshire Railway Station, c.1896. This became the Great Central Railway Station in 1897. The horse and carriage was from Parson's Livery on Soresby Street.

Market Place Station, West Bars, 1952.

This photograph of the Midland Railway Station, c.1900s, shows carriages waiting to transport passengers from the station.

The Ashover Carrier at Chesterfield, Lancashire, Derbyshire & East Coast Railway Station, c.1897–1907.

The Flying Scotsman *at Chesterfield in the late 1960s.*

Steam locomotive (63594) class '01' with empty coal wagons on Staveley's Central Railway Line, pre-1964.

The interior of the North Junction railway signal box at Staveley, c.1950.

Relaying the track at Barrow Hill, 1936.

British Rail Station, formerly the Midland Railway Station. The station was altered and refurbished in 2001.

TRAMS AND TROLLEYBUSES – PUBLIC TRANSPORT IN CHESTERFIELD

The growth and expansion of Chesterfield led to the development of tram and later bus services in and around the town. The Chesterfield and District Tramways Company was formed in December 1881 and in October 1882 it launched a regular horse-drawn service between Brampton and the town centre. A few weeks later the route between Brampton and Walton commenced operation. From the outset, however, the enterprise faced considerable difficulties. This was a private company with only limited resources, and with only three trams and 12 horses it struggled to survive. The company found it difficult to recruit competent staff and was soon beset with problems of poor timekeeping and general unreliability. This, in turn, resulted in financial problems and in 1886 it was forced into voluntary liquidation. The service was rescued by a group of local businessmen who purchased the whole undertaking and formed a new company – Chesterfield Tramways. Two additional trams were purchased and the company seemed to fare better than its predecessor. In 1897, however, the whole undertaking was purchased by Chesterfield Corporation for the sum of £2,050. A Tramways sub-committee was established to oversee the operation of the tramway network and an immediate decision was made to reduce fares from 2d to 1d. This was a popular decision in the town but resulted in overcrowding at certain times of the day and requests for an increase in the frequency of the service. To meet this demand the Corporation acquired a further three trams between 1897 and 1898.

The tramway prospered under Corporation management and in addition to fares it also obtained revenue from the sale of advertising on both tickets and the trams themselves. Two more trams were purchased in 1899 but by this time the Corporation was already beginning to consider the possibility of electrification. Such a scheme required parliamentary approval but on 23 June 1904 the Chesterfield Corporation Tramways and Improvements Act received the Royal Assent. Twelve electric trams were purchased from

A horse-drawn tram in 1881.

Chesterfield's old and new trams, 1905-06. This photograph shows the new double-decker electric tramcar and the old horse tram side by side.

Chesterfield's last tram and first trolleybus, 1927.

An electric tram towing a trailer at Whittington Moor, c.1910.

Chesterfield's last electric tramcar run, 1927.

Girdham's Charabanc outside the Crown Hotel, Market Street, Staveley, c.1926.

An early Hulley's bus, 1922. Hulley's provided a service between Chesterfield and Barlow in the 1920s.

Chesterfield Corporation Transport buses passing each other on Saltergate, c.1940s.

The Corporation Transport Department headquarters on Sheffield Road, 1966. Demolition took place shortly after Stagecoach took over the running of the buses.

Modern TM Travel Coach photographed outside the pavements shopping centre, 2009.

The bus station on New Beetwell Street in 2002.

A bass drummer of the Sherwood Foresters, c.1909.

A drum major of the Sherwood Foresters, c.1909.

The 2nd Volunteer Battalion of the Sherwood Foresters marching along Saltergate.

Derbyshire Yeomanry in Chesterfield Market Place, early 1900s.

Derbyshire Yeomanry marching along Brewery Street.

Ashover Territorials in the yard of the Drill Hall, Ashgate Road, Chesterfield, c.1908.

Civil Defence personnel marching past the Nags Head on Chesterfield Road, Staveley, 8 May 1945 (VE Day).

The British Legion laying a wreath at the War Memorial by Revolution House, Old Whittington, c.1950.

THE NEW MILLENNIUM – CHESTERFIELD LOOKS TOWARDS THE FUTURE

Considerable changes and improvements have been made to Chesterfield in the 21st century and the whole town now exudes a confident and vibrant atmosphere. The hospital is one of the most modern and well equipped in the country and the concern for helping people develop a healthy lifestyle was reflected in the opening of the new Healthy Living Centre at Staveley in 2008. A number of other public buildings have also been built or modernised since the Millennium. A new courthouse was built on Tapton Lane in 2004. The railway station was extensively modernised in 2005 and a statue of George Stephenson was erected outside the main entrance in the same year. In 2006 a new community fire station was opened at Staveley.

Local schools continue to provide a high standard of education and several have been rebuilt or extended since 2000. At Springwell Community School, Staveley, for example, a new performing arts centre was built in 2005 and two years later a sports centre with dance studio and fitness centre was added. The rest of the school is due to be rebuilt on the current site during 2009–10. The plans envisage three, two-tier 'strawberry-shaped pods', which are intended to maximise learning space. When completed in Autumn 2010 the school will provide accommodation for 850 students aged 11–16 as well as 20 more places for post-16 students who wish to pursue more advanced courses.

The employment structure of the town has also continued to change. A number of the older engineering companies such as Bryan Donkin and Markham and Co. have disappeared. Unemployment remains high but new employers are being encouraged to

The Markham Works in the process of demolition.

The statue of George Stephenson outside the railway station.

settle in the town. In planning for the future the borough council has identified a number of sites for industrial development. New business units have been created at Markham Vale and elsewhere in the borough. A good example of these business units is Prospect House, which opened at the Ireland Business Park in 2006. This high-quality, two-tier development was specifically aimed at technology businesses.

The increasing importance of tourism in the area was reflected in the building of a new tourist information centre. Opened in November 2002, the building's octagonal shape reflects the eight sides of the spire on the parish church. A number of new hotels have recently been built and the council sees the further development of the Chesterfield Canal as an important asset in the encouragement of tourism. A town trail and accompanying audio tour has also been developed to help visitors explore the town.

The retail structure of Chesterfield continues to change and develop. The Vicar Lane shopping centre was opened in 2000 but other stores have closed. Partly as a result of the 'Credit Crunch', the Woolworth's chain went into liquidation in 2008 and in December of that year the Chesterfield store closed its doors for the last time. The Borough Local Plan recognised that 'the attractiveness of Chesterfield town centre is partly due to its traditional character, based around a popular market and a range of smaller independent shops complementing the multiple larger national stores'. It also identified the need for a large DIY retail warehouse to serve the whole Chesterfield catchment area, and in April 2009 a large B&Q store was opened on the former Donkin/UEF site on Derby Road.

The political landscape of the town has also changed considerably in recent years. For decades a Labour stronghold, and the seat of veteran politician Tony Benn, the Chesterfield constituency elected Liberal Democrat Paul Holmes as its MP in 2001. At the time of writing the Liberal Democrats also control the borough council. The political pendulum will almost certainly continue to swing in the years to come but undoubtedly the social demography of the town has changed. The 21st century has also seen single-issue groups and campaigning charities becoming more important. A number of trade unions, community organisations and charities flourish within the town. Some of these organisations were involved in Chesterfield's efforts to become a Fairtrade Town; a status which it achieved in 2009.

While looking to the future, Chesterfield is also concerned to preserve its heritage. A number of buildings, including the Winding Wheel Conference Centre, have been granted listed building status. Throughout the town distinctive blue plaques identify historic buildings such as the Cannon Mill and The Falcon Building. The Chesterfield Townscape Heritage Initiative is a grant scheme for properties in the centre of Chesterfield which aims to regenerate both the historic fabric and the economy of the town centre. Grants are also available for the reinstatement of architectural features such as the façades of buildings, upper-floor windows and decorative cast-iron rainwater pipes. The next generation have also been involved in this project and local schools have been engaged in fieldwork and surveys.

In the 21st century there is deep concern about biodiversity and the future of the environment. As a result the borough council commissioned Derbyshire Wildlife Trust to produce 'A Greenprint for Chesterfield'. Published in 2003, this document set out a vision for biodiversity in Chesterfield as a place where:

The importance of the natural environment to the quality of life of Chesterfield's people is recognised by everyone;

A network of wildlife habitats exists throughout the borough;

Everyone works together to protect and enhance biodiversity, creating a brighter, more sustainable future;

People can learn about and enjoy the natural environment and are given every opportunity through the provision of accessible, local, natural green space.

A number of policies have been put in place to turn this vision into reality, and in particular action is being taken to protect a number of locally endangered species including the water vole, the skylark and the grass snake.

Some parts of the borough have faced more difficulties than others in recent years and Staveley in particular has struggled to come to terms with problems associated with the disappearance of mining and the decline of heavy industry. In 2002, however, the township was chosen to be a pilot pathfinder project for the Neighbourhood Renewal Unit. Funded by the Office of the Deputy Prime Minister (ODPM) the Staveley Neighbourhood Management Project was set up in 2002 and aimed to 'address the difficulties associated with the decline of traditional industries and improve services by bringing together services providers and the community to deliver services in a better, more co-ordinated and responsive way'. Although the project was wound-up in September 2009, it achieved a great deal in regenerating and revitalising the area. It sponsored or co-ordinated a huge range of projects and activities including the setting-up of a toy library, the creation of community allotments and the restoration of parts of the Chesterfield Canal. Other activities focussed on the reduction of crime, improvements in school attendance and the encouragement of a healthier lifestyle. Demonstrable success was achieved in all these areas, and in 2006 a national conference was held at Ringwood Hall at which representatives of organisations from all over the country came to learn from the success of the Staveley Project.

The newsletter distributed by Staveley Neighbourhood Management Project was called *Buzz*. This was an appropriate title for there is certainly a buzz about Chesterfield today. Changes and improvements are being made throughout the town with new houses, shops, schools and business premises being built every year. Chesterfield is clearly a town with a great future and a proud past.

The New Tourist Information Centre under construction in 2002. The Tourist Information Centre was relocated from the Peacock Centre and the area was renamed Rykneld Square.

Ravenside Retail Park, 2009.

Markham Works in the process of demolition, 2001.

The construction of New Court House on Durant Road, 2002.

The new housing development on Old School Close, Holymoorside, 2004.

The New School on Holy Moor Road, Holymoorside, 2004.

Modern appartments near the centre of Chesterfield.

The new Tourist Information Centre in 2009.

The new B&Q store photographed just prior to its opening in April 2009.

The recently modernised Chesterfield Railway Station.

Modern housing at Barrow Hill.

The Barrow Roundhouse Railway Centre contributes to the tourist industry in the area.

Hollingwood Lock on the Chesterfield Canal, 2009. The borough council sees the preservation and development of the Chesterfield Canal as an important part of its strategy for developing tourism in the area.

The Sun Inn. A traditional pub with modern entertainment, 2009.

The children's play area at Poolsbrook Country Park, 2009.

Prospect House, Ireland Business Park, 2009.

Markham Vale Environment Centre, 2009.

Select Bibliography

Basson, S. *Chesterfield FC — The Official Story* Harefield, 2000.

Becket, J.V. *The East Midlands from AD 1000* London, 1988.

Bestall, J.M. *History of Chesterfield, Vol I: Early and Medieval Chesterfield* Chesterfield, 1974.

Bestall, J.M. and Fowkes, D.V. *History of Chesterfield, Vol. II Part 2 — Restoration and Georgian Chesterfield* Chesterfield, 1984.

Bestall, J.M. and Fowkes, D.V. *History of Chesterfield: Vol. III — Early Victorian Chesterfield* Chesterfield, 1978.

Chapman, S.D. *Stanton and Staveley* Cambridge, 1981.

Chesterfield Borough Council *Commercial Chesterfield* Chesterfield, 1931.

Cooper, R. *The Book of Chesterfield* Buckingham, 1977.

Court *Staveley — My Native Town* Sheffield, 1988.

Fiennes, C. (ed. C. Morris) *Journeys* London, 1976.

Finney, M. *Men of Iron* Chesterfield, 1995.

Ford, T. *The History of Chesterfield* Chesterfield, 1839.

Hall, G. *The History of Chesterfield* Chesterfield, 1823.

Hey, D. *Derbyshire, a History* Lancaster, 2008.

Pendleton, J. and Jacques, W. *Modern Chesterfield* Chesterfield, 1906.

Marsden, B.M. *Chesterfield Trams and Trolleybuses* Chesterfield, 1984.

Morgan, P. (ed.) *Domesday Book, Phillimore Series Vol. XXVII Derbyshire* Chichester, 1978.

Nixon, F. *The Industrial Archaeology of Derbyshire* Newton Abbott, 1969.

Page, W. (ed.) *The Victoria History of the County of Derby* London, 1907 (2 Vols).

Pevsner, N. *The Buildings of England: Derbyshire* London, 1953.

Riden, P. *History of Chesterfield, Vol. II Part 1: Tudor and Stuart Chesterfield* Chesterfield, 1984.

Robinson, P. *The Smiths of Chesterfield* Chesterfield, 1957.

Roques, L.P. *The Story of the Spital* Chesterfield, 2008.

Sadler, G. (ed) *Aspects of Chesterfield — Discovering Local History* Barnsley, 2002.

Smith, M.E. *Derbyshire Canals* Derby, 1987.

Smith, M.E. *Industrial Derbyshire* Derby, 2008.

Stone, B. *Derbyshire in the Civil War* Cromford, 1992.

Stones, S.H. *Whittington and the Glorious Revolution* Sheffield, 1988.

Turbutt, G. *A History of Derbyshire* Whitchurch, 1999 (4 Vols).

White, P. *The Robinson Story 1839–2000* Chesterfield, 2000.

Wort, K.G. and Bennett, M.G. *Markham & Company of Chesterfield, 1889–1998* Whitchurch, 2005.

Wright, T.F. *History of Chesterfield, Vol. IV: The Development of the Modern Town, 1851–1939* Chesterfield, 1992.

A wide range of primary sources have also been consulted including yearbooks, directories, local council publications and newspapers. Chesterfield Museum has also been a useful source of information. A number of websites have yielded valuable material, particularly 'Picture the Past'.